"People need to be more productive in tl  ir
stress levels and stop simply reacting. Eve el
of their lives. I am a firm believer in str u
step by step. This book's Peak Productivi e
this next step in all aspects of your life."

—Christian Barbosa, CEO, Triad Productivity Solutions

The Secret to Peak Productivity provides a new innovative approach to reaching goals and 'possibilities' in all areas of life. Tamara Myles has done an outstanding job in offering specific guidance for completing each step necessary to attaining successes. She provides the reader with clear explanations, examples, and outlines of the steps that are necessary to complete in order to advance to the next step in this ongoing process.

This is an easy read, and unlike many books, the author's style reflects her message: It is lucid, offers direction, and leads the reader to the goal of realizing true possibilities. This book will definitely be on my list of resources offered to my clients."

—Rosanne Lowe, R.N., Ph.D., Psychologist, Certified Positive
Psychology Coach, Wellness Consultant and Coach

"This is a book I will keep close for reference for years to come. Owning my own business over the last twelve years had unnecessarily stolen some of my 'inner peace,' which comes from accomplishing day-to-day responsibilities with ease. Thanks to Tamara's manageable organizational system, I have already begun to put the Peak Productivity Pyramid System into effect. Tamara's 'Three To's' and 'Email ABC's' have already started a major decluttering process!"

—Eileen Rappold, Owner/Director, Personal Best Karate, Easton, MA

"What a valuable and unique system Tamara has created and has generously shared with all of us. The Productivity Pyramid will, I repeat, *will* change the way you work and live for the better! Simplifying our work and life using the Peak Productivity Pyramid is a gift that Tamara is sharing with all of us. Be sure to accept this gift.

I have personally benefitted an enormous amount because of this book and Tamara's insights. In order for me to describe all of the benefits that have occurred because of reading it, I would need to write my own book!"

—John James Allaire Jr., Realtor®, Broker,
Owner, Easton Real Estate, Easton, MA

"Tamara Myles presents the steps to organizing life and work activities for success in a simple-to-understand process with her Peak Productivity Pyramid. I highly recommend reading her book, for even if you think you are already a master at organizing—you'll learn something new."

—Maureen Wilkinson, VP & Director *HarborOne U*

"*The Secret to Peak Productivity* offers a unique blend of organizing and productivity theory and a pragmatic, practical approach to organizing your business and personal life. Read the book. Commit the Pyramid to memory. If you implement just one tip from this book, you will see immediate results and be making a step toward many possibilities in life."

—Ellen M. Bruno, CPA/PFS, CGMA, President,
Compliance Advisor Professionals, LLC

"Tamara's book offers a comprehensive solution for the productivity challenges we all face. Her clear and logical approach is easy to understand and is sure to resonate with business professionals and any individual striving to maximize her or his potential. She leaves you with an actionable, step-by-step plan to follow, which is every productivity consultant's dream resource."

—Wendy Buglio, Certified Professional Organizer®, Functional Places®

"This book was inspirational and very easy to read. It is truly a valuable reminder of those important focus points that all of us with way too much to do and too little time to do it can use to keep our productivity at its highest level. I have seen the members of the Women's Business Network of SE MA utilize portions of Tamara's system in organizing their physical offices, as well as to help them implement their own goals in a more productive way with their electronic systems. Tamara offers many solutions that business owners will easily be able to use right away. Now that I have read this book once, I will be reading it again and again to continue to fine-tune my own productivity strategies."

—Susan Finn, Founder/Director of the Women's Business Network of SE MA

"After reading just the first few chapters of *The Secret to Peak Productivity*, I got inspired to become more organized, efficient, productive, and satisfied at work. I loved the book. It was an easy read; insightful and motivating. Instead of feeling bad about the lack of organization in my life, it made me feel excited about the possibilities. I decided the most important thing I can do for myself and my team is to give each staff member a copy of this book. Thanks to Tamara for the incentive to get back on track."

—Cheryl Opper, Founder and Executive Director,
School on Wheels of Massachusetts

"Implementing Tamara's Peak Productivity Pyramid System has helped me streamline my workday and makes me feel more in control of my business. While interruptions will always occur, having a structure in place has helped minimize distractions, put focus on the most important tasks, and keeps my business moving forward."

—Katy Argenzio, Owner of Anytime Fitness, Easton, MA

THE SECRET TO
PEAK
PRODUCTIVITY

A Simple Guide to Reaching
Your Personal Best

Tamara Myles

AMACOM

AMERICAN MANAGEMENT ASSOCIATION

New York • Atlanta • Brussels • Chicago • Mexico City • San Francisco
Shanghai • Tokyo • Toronto • Washington, D.C.

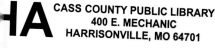

Bulk discounts available. For details visit: www.amacombooks.org/go/specialsales
Or contact special sales: Phone: 800-250-5308 E-mail: specialsls@amanet.org
View all the AMACOM titles at: www.amacombooks.org
American Management Association: www.amanet.org

This publication is designed to provide accurate and authoritative information in regard to the subject matter covered. It is sold with the understanding that the publisher is not engaged in rendering legal, accounting, or other professional service. If legal advice or other expert assistance is required, the services of a competent professional person should be sought.

LIBRARY OF CONGRESS CATALOGING-IN-PUBLICATION DATA
Myles, Tamara Schwambach Kano.
The secret to peak productivity : a simple guide to reaching your personal best / Tamara Schwambach Kano Myles.
pages cm
Includes bibliographical references and index.
ISBN 978-0-8144-3385-0 (pbk. : alk. paper)—ISBN 0-8144-3385-5 (pbk. : alk. paper)
1. Time management. 2. Orderliness. 3. Performance. I. Title.
HD69.T54M96 2014
650.1'1—dc23   2013033619

About AMA
American Management Association (www.amanet.org) is a world leader in talent development, advancing the skills of individuals to drive business success. Our mission is to support the goals of individuals and organizations through a complete range of products and services, including classroom and virtual seminars, webcasts, webinars, podcasts, conferences, corporate and government solutions, business books, and research. AMA's approach to improving performance combines experiential learning—learning through doing—with opportunities for ongoing professional growth at every step of one's career journey.

Printing number

10 9 8 7 6 5 4 3 2 1

To Isabella, Eddie, and Viviana,
may you always strive to create possibility in your life.

CONTENTS

14. CASE STUDY: JOHN ALLAIRE

FIGURES AND TABLES

ACKNOWLEDGMENTS

So many people have helped me along the way while I was growing my business and developing the professional expertise that has made this book possible. To everyone I do not mention individually, please know that I am very grateful. To the following people and organizations, I offer my deepest and most heartfelt appreciation.

To all of my clients, for giving me the experiences that have helped me learn along the way, for the relationships, friendships, and pleasure of working with them. Especially to those clients whose stories have helped to inform this book.

To all of the many productivity experts who have influenced my work. And Benjamin Zander, for his inspiring talk that set me on the path to possibility. To Maslow, for helping me to make sense out of the progressive nature of productivity, which I've experienced working with clients.

To the many associations and organizations that have helped me along the way, especially to the Women's Business Network of Southeastern Massachusetts; for the business relationships, friendships, and encouragement of Susan Finn and my other colleagues in that group; and to the New England chapter of the National Association of Professional Organizers, especially the women on the board with whom I served for two years, for their encouragement, inspiration, and trusted advice.

To Maureen Wilkinson at HarborOne U, for giving me so many opportunities to share my knowledge with a variety of business and educational groups, along with the television experience and recognition that it brings.

To the many who have helped me develop my business, including my small-business adviser, Tricia White, who helps me with so many different aspects, including developing my business plan, and business consultant Irene Buchine, who helped me clarify my marketing strategy.

To Claudia Gere, my brilliant writer and literary agent, who guided me throughout the book writing and publishing process, who made the dream of writing a book a reality and more rewarding than I thought possible.

To Ellen Kadin, my editor, and the amazing production, marketing, and sales teams at AMACOM Books, who brought my book to life and have given it the best opportunity for success I could hope for.

To my early readers, including Ted, Emily, Daniela, Jayson, and Rachel, for taking the time to read my manuscript and offering valuable insights, comments, and suggestions. To my friends and neighbors because, as most everyone knows, it takes a village to raise a family, and in many ways it's the same for raising a business. Thank you for helping me balance a business and family, by being there to talk to, taking the kids for playdates, or greeting them at the bus stop. Thank you to everyone for being my village.

To my extended family in Brazil: my grandparents, aunts, uncles, and cousins for their love, support, and enrichment of my life.

To the wonderful family that surrounds me with love and support:

my sister-in-law Rachel, an internationally trained, world-class stylist (rachellefort.com), for adding pizzazz to my style for a professional and fashionable look.

To my brother-in-law Brian, for all his help with writing and reviewing contracts and for helping to secure trademarks and copyrights.

To my mother-in-law, Emily, for encouraging me to listen to and follow my heart, and then being there to care for the children, when I need her to, so I can.

To my brother Eduardo, for all of his support, especially for launching and hosting my website, as well as his excellent IT skills that have helped me keep my business running smoothly.

To my sister Daniela, my best friend, who is always there for me, knowing intuitively the moment when I need her to call me for support or advice.

To my parents, Sergio and Adelina, for encouraging and believing in me and providing such love and support that I had no choice but to always believe in myself. I owe what I am today to them.

To my husband, Ted, for always believing in me and, with his keen business sense, encouraging and challenging me to take this business to another level; for his love and emotional support along our great journey together; and for the most important thing in my life, this beautiful family of ours.

THE SECRET TO
PEAK PRODUCTIVTY

CHAPTER 1

STEPS TO PRODUCTIVITY

W hat distinguishes a professional organizer or productivity consultant from a decluttering or cleaning service? Professional organizers transfer skills rather than simply complete tasks. You might pick up a handy tip or two from an office cleaning service, but that is not their goal. Office cleaners do not want to transfer skills or offer tools and train their way out of a job.

At every client appointment, professional organizers strive to transfer skills, teach systems, and explain processes. They are committed to empowering their clients with the necessary skills to achieve their best organization system. Empowerment is always top of mind because consultants want their clients to achieve success. Success only happens when consultants explain systems and processes in a way that helps their clients organize their environments in their own way, and a way that works for them.

One of my earliest clients, Cindy, called me, saying, "My office is a disaster. I need you to come help me organize my office. Things have gotten so crazy that I am in the office every night until eleven o'clock. I'm just trying to catch up with what's happened that day, and I never get to the piles of papers around me. I need to feel in control, and I think everything will be okay if I can just dig out from under all of this paper."

When I arrived for my appointment with Cindy, I found a small bedroom that she had turned into her office. She had a desk with a computer, phone, and an inbox on it. Across from the desk were wall shelves, and there was a filing cabinet. The doors of the closet had been removed. All I could see were piles of papers. They were stacked on the desk, on top of the filing cabinet, on the wall shelves, on the floor, as well as piled in the closet.

We started working, and it was clear to me, just from the first half hour of my assessment, that it wasn't just papers causing her problems. She had a time management problem as well. The papers were a side effect, a symptom of larger problems, but it was the piles of papers that bothered her. The most common reason people call me is because they think they need help getting their physical space organized, the clutter of papers, books, and other materials in the office. Usually, they cannot see the whole picture because they are focused on the symptoms, and that's what triggers them to call. The physical clutter gets to the point where it's too much, and it is too overwhelming and becomes stressful. That's why Cindy called.

Very gently, I shared my observations. "You know, paper is often a symptom of bigger issues," I said. We looked at her calendar book and her system to keep track of tasks. There were Post-it notes everywhere, and notes on other pieces of paper stuck with tape or propped next to the telephone. She did not have a system to keep track of calls. If somebody left a message and she needed to return the call, she put a Post-it on her computer screen, desktop, or phone handle to remind herself. There were piles and piles of papers, including especially important files that she couldn't lose. The first thing we tackled was the physical clutter.

Nearly 90 percent of the people who call for help initiate that first call because they feel overwhelmed by physical clutter. Some clients are happiest to have someone come in and clean up their offices, file their papers, make everything look tidy, leaving them with an office that's cleaner. Others welcome the opportunity to find a lasting solution for managing their incoming papers, mail, and other documents. In other words, some clients call and want a Band-Aid for the symptom; others are ready to endeavor to find the root cause of the issue so that they can become empowered to develop lasting solutions to their productivity issues. One thing became apparent to me over the years working as a professional organizer: It was rare that anyone was ready to deal with the other issues, such as electronic clutter and time management, until a person's physical clutter was brought under control.

When I discovered that there was a flow to introducing the various strategies for achieving physical organization, electronic organization, and so on, I was excited. It felt as though I had made a novel discovery. Sitting across from my husband explaining my findings, I was sounding him out on suggestions for how I could explain this process to my prospective clients. He quietly said, "You've heard of Maslow's pyramid, haven't you?"

MASLOW'S PYRAMID

Unless you've been to business school to study management, or studied psychology, sociology, or another field that focuses on human behavior, you are probably only casually aware of Maslow's hierarchy of needs. Like me, you probably haven't spent a lot of time applying his theories in the real world. In his 1943 psychological research studies on what motivates people, Abraham Maslow discovered there is a logical order of needs that have to be satisfied before people can be motivated to the next level. He identified five levels, starting with the most essential needs:

1. *Physiological.* The most basic needs that people experience are the essentials for their survival, such as air, food, drink, shelter, sex,

and sleep. They need to satisfy these needs before they are motivated to be concerned about the next level.

2. *Safety.* Once people's physiological needs are met, then security becomes important, including personal and financial security, health, and well-being.

3. *Love and Belonging.* Next in the hierarchy of needs that motivate us are relationships, such as work, group, family, and partner.

4. *Esteem.* Both self-esteem and respect from others are among the needs identified in the next level.

5. *Self-Actualization.* The highest level that motivates people is fulfilling their greatest potential.

Most often Maslow's hierarchy of needs is expressed as a pyramid with the most essential needs expressed in the lowest level. Figure 1-1 illustrates his philosophy of the relationship between the different types of needs. For example, people who don't feel loved or a sense of belonging (level 3) will not have self-esteem or feel respected by others (level 4). You cannot convince people to possess self-esteem unless they achieve the love and belonging needs in the third level first. People need to fulfill each level, starting with physiological needs, before being motivated to move up the pyramid and achieve the next level.

The strategy for fulfilling a more productive life follows a similar pattern. People have to satisfy, to some extent, competency with one level before they can move on to the next. That led me to create a structure that mirrors Maslow's pyramid, using what I have learned working with so many clients to help them improve and enhance their productivity. It's called the Peak Productivity Pyramid™ system.

THE PRODUCTIVITY PYRAMID

The Peak Productivity Pyramid™ System defines the motivational relationship among five areas of productivity. It is a holistic and comprehen-

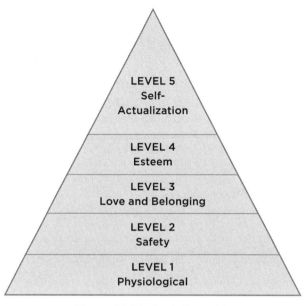

Figure 1-1. Maslow's Pyramid.

sive approach to productivity that starts with streamlining your basic organizational systems and moving up the pyramid, working toward developing goals for different possibilities in your life. The Peak Productivity Pyramid System is a unique and proven framework to take people who want to improve their productivity through the journey of aligning their daily activities to their goals and objectives.

Here are the Peak Productivity Pyramid's five levels, starting with the first level:

1. *Physical Organization.* The process begins with managing the accumulation of documents, magazines, mail, notes, and books. In the business world, this is the primary need that draws people into improving their productivity.

2. *Electronic Organization.* Having systems in place for handling your online information—all the different ways we have to

communicate, store, and retrieve information electronically—is essential to success at the next level.

3. *Time Management.* This is the most common need associated with productivity. Time management involves managing tasks and appointments, to-do lists, calendars, and what you do in a given day.

4. *Activity-Goal Alignment.* The tasks at this level are setting goals, both business and personal, and then aligning what you do each day to fulfill those goals.

5. *Possibility.* Similar to self-actualization in the Maslow hierarchy, the fifth level of the Peak Productivity Pyramid is the culmination of mastering the previous four levels. Level 5 is not something to be achieved or a place to be; rather, possibility is the continual examination and goal-setting process on the path to fulfilling your potential.

The Peak Productivity Pyramid illustrates the way people approach productivity level by level. Although it is a series of five levels, the Peak Productivity Pyramid (see Figure 1-2) is not always exclusively a linear path. Given the busyness of our lives, the distractions we experience, and how our physical and electronic worlds are constantly evolving, there will always be ways to improve productivity.

Even after mastering a productivity level, it is helpful to revisit each level occasionally. It's easy to backslide and fall into old habits, especially when life gets extremely busy. It's important to check whether you continue to implement the systems you have in place. Other times you might want to backslide on purpose. You may need to reassess whether the systems you have in place are meeting your current needs. Particularly with the speed at which technology evolves, a tool that worked very well for a while could be made obsolete by a new app or program that better aligns with your methods of managing electronic information or your time. New strategies and capabilities introduce new tactics for increasing

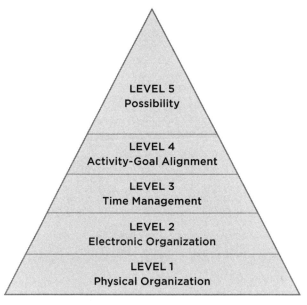

Figure 1-2. Productivity Pyramid.

your productivity. As the scope of your goals and the resulting activities change, you might need different systems to accommodate those differences in what you do.

In most cases, when I start working with a client, the most pressing needs for improving productivity are quickly apparent. The exact needs and the outcome will be as varied as the people who undertake their own journey toward peak productivity. Not every path is a smooth one.

THE CHALLENGE OF CHANGE

Cindy was very challenged by change. A short time after our initial project together, her business expanded and she was preparing to move from her home office into a professional office park. She asked for my help in setting up her new environment before the move, so that it would be ready to handle her expanding business needs.

To start, we set up a well-planned physical structure, using shelving, filing cabinets, and other storage containers. We revisited systems for sorting and filing documents. We looked at the business's electronic files and established filing systems that mirrored their physical counterparts. We created a shared electronic calendar for all employees and developed processes and systems for training new hires. When we finished, it was a state-of-the-art business setup.

It wasn't long, though, before Cindy called and told me that she needed more help. Once again she was buried by physical clutter, her e-mail and electronic scheduling systems were disorganized, and she was failing to execute effectively on her business deliverables. My first reaction was to assume that the systems we'd chosen weren't working for her, but upon further analysis it was clear that she just wasn't ready to embrace change. The lesson learned is that unless you are ready for change, and are willing to implement and learn the systems you put in place, the papers will continue to pile up, e-mail will continue to overwhelm you, and deadlines will continually be missed. Unless you commit to the process, you may never find out what other changes would help you to be more productive and help you achieve your greater goals.

CLIMBING THE PEAK PRODUCTIVITY PYRAMID LEVELS

I met John when I first moved into town. He was a forty-year-old successful entrepreneur, and we hit it off right away, so we stayed in touch.

By coincidence, he approached me with some networking ideas just as I was transitioning my business from residential organizing to business productivity training. Before he could introduce me and my services to the community, John wanted to learn more about my business and what I do. As I explained how I had been helping several clients achieve greater productivity, he was quite direct with me and said, "I don't think there is anything you could do for me, though. I'm on top of my goals;

I'm so organized. I'm very type A, you know." This confidence and directness is one of the many reasons John and I get along so well. I did, however, see his candor as a direct challenge and an intriguing opportunity. Does the Peak Productivity Pyramid System only work for people with acute problems, or could I actually help a high-performing person reach the possibility level?

At our first meeting in his office, I asked him, "Okay, show me. How do you organize your day? And what do you do in a day? What scheduling systems do you use?"

When John showed me how he kept track of his appointments and followed up with clients, one of his routine tasks jumped out at me as being overly complex. I made a quick suggestion that he implemented right away. That one change saved him two hours a week. Since John puts a high value on his time and assesses what it's worth, two hours per week was a serious time savings.

"Well, maybe we should work together," he suggested.

John has been a steady client ever since. While the frequency of our interactions vary, based on where he is in his business cycle, John does hold continuous improvement as a top priority in his business and personal life. Because I saw firsthand that his office was immaculate, we skipped the first level of productivity improvement, physical organization, and began at level 2, electronic organization.

Even though he was extremely organized electronically to handle his e-mail and schedule, we implemented techniques that streamlined some of the ways he was managing other electronic information. Being more efficient is very appealing to a type A personality such as John. He is always striving to be better, to be his best.

When we tackled level 3, time management, we worked specifically on delegation. His work on delegation was essential to support his activity-goal alignment (level 4). John had been so focused on his business that he hadn't set goals for his personal life and his relationships. He spent time with his family, but there were other areas he hadn't been paying attention to. One of his primary goals was to reduce his work-week from fifty hours to thirty hours while maintaining the same level of productivity, so he could spend time on those other aspects of his life.

Today, no one knows he's only working in his business thirty hours a week, but he is. He is delegating much more than he used to, and as a result, he no longer works on weekends. When he reached his goal, I asked him, "Now that you're working thirty hours a week, what are you going to do with the newly found twenty hours? If you don't have a pur-pose, then you're going to waste them with stuff you have no idea you're even doing."

That was when he reached level 5—*possibility*. Part of the exercise of possibility was sitting down with him and doing time logs so that he could clearly see where his time was going. Once he knew how he was using the time, he could then shift those hours to what he wanted to do. But first he needed to figure out how to use the twenty hours. What new activities would fill that available time? Once he figured that out, he could align his activities to his goals. Now he knows that he will use the time for his spiritual activities, journaling, relationships, and other spe-cific, important activities he didn't have time for before. That was John's path to possibility.

Possibility, or achieving your full potential, is always a work in prog-ress. You need to examine your goals often enough to be sure they are still what you want, and that there aren't new, more important goals. It is easy to fall into old patterns and behaviors, backsliding away from what is most important to you. You can read John's full story, from his perspective, in the last chapter of this book.

There are several lessons to learn from John's experience:

* You can't always be sure what level is the best place to start. Where do you have mastery and where can you learn new skills that will help you be more productive?

- Even when you think you have mastered a level, there will be other skills to learn that will make you more productive. The path isn't always linear, moving directly up the pyramid. It is a good idea to check in periodically at each level to see if you are being as efficient as you can be.
- Possibility and activity-goal alignment are iterative processes and part of a continuous exercise to be certain you are achieving your ultimate goals.

Not everyone starts at the first level. Everyone has different primary and secondary needs for improving productivity, which is why people will move through the levels at their own pace. For those who review and hone their skills throughout the first four levels, the payoff of achieving peak productivity is worth it. People need to address the first four levels of productivity before they can access the possibility level, and once they do, they will be open to business-changing, life-changing opportunities.

Reaching the possibility level means that instead of always responding to crises, you have your life in control. You are working on what is most important for you to accomplish your goals in an environment that is organized and supports your best work. The first step is to figure out what you need to improve. That is, which level of the Peak Productivity Pyramid should you start with on your path to peak productivity?

PRODUCTIVITY POINTERS

- Just like Maslow's hierarchy of needs, the Peak Productivity Pyramid System recognizes that people need to fulfill each level before being able to advance successfully to the next.
- There is no right level for beginning your journey; you need to discover *your* productivity strengths and weaknesses to find the right level for you to start.

- Everyone's journey will be different. The process can be iterative and learning will be continuous.
- Before climbing the Peak Productivity Pyramid, you must be ready for change; nothing will happen without being ready to replace what is not working with something that will work.

CHAPTER 2

WHERE TO START

W hy did you buy this book? If I could ask you questions right now, that would be the first one. You could tell me what has brought you to this point of looking for ways to improve your productivity.

- Are you drowning in physical clutter?
- Has your e-mail inbox overwhelmed you?
- Do you feel you should be accomplishing more in any given day?
- Do your business and life goals seem out of reach?
- Do you have aspirations that you know you can achieve once you get control of your life?
- Are you looking for the innovative edge that will help you improve your already excellent skills?

Questions like these help us identify our strengths, weaknesses, and areas for improvement. Because I can't ask you these questions in person, and because a book on productivity should be as efficient as possible, I've created an assessment to help you examine which areas of productivity improvement will benefit you the most. Focusing on those areas first will lead to improvements faster.

PEAK PRODUCTIVITY PYRAMID ASSESSMENT

Complete the Peak Productivity Pyramid Assessment, shown in Table 2-1. After you read the book and implement the advice that makes the most sense for you, you can retake the assessment to see how you have improved in the different areas. You will be able to measure the return on investment of your time in reading this book.

Taking the assessment is a simple process of answering each of the 32 questions by putting a check mark in the column (column 1, 2, or 3) that corresponds to your best answer. After completing each of the sections, you need to tally the number of check marks in columns 1, 2, and 3. At the end, you review the results of your choices within each section. None of the responses to these questions will be perfect. To make it as easy as possible, don't think too hard about the answer that is most like you; go with your honest, first instinct. Think about your life as it is right now, not the person you were or want to become. Answer by selecting the statement that best describes your actual behavior.

SCORING YOUR ASSESSMENT

Once you have completed the assessment in Table 2-1, compile your scores using the tally sheet shown in Table 2-2, and then read on to see where you excel and where you can work to improve your productivity. The following explanations will help you interpret the results of your assessment and allow you to focus your efforts so that you can get the most out of this book.

TABLE 2-1. PEAK PRODUCTIVITY PYRAMID ASSESSMENT

LEVEL 1: PHYSICAL ORGANIZATION	1 ✔	2 ✔	3 ✔
When you look around your office, you see:			
1. Stacks of random papers on surfaces and floors			
2. A few small piles on the desk or other work surfaces			
3. Clear work spaces and surfaces			
I use a filing container for my papers.			
1. Not really			
2. Yes, a traditional letter cabinet and/or standing files			
3. Yes, a mix of file containers that works best for my needs and space			
I use a system for sorting my papers.			
1. Not really			
2. Yes, alphabetically, chronologically, or by category			
3. Yes, one of the above, plus further sorting systems			
I sort and file my papers.			
1. Rarely, if ever			
2. When I find the time			
3. Frequently and on a regular basis			
I've considered different kinds of systems for filing my papers.			
1. Rarely, if ever			
2. Sometimes			
3. Yes, I know a wide variety of filing systems			
Tally the check marks in the 1, 2, and 3 columns.			

LEVEL 2: ELECTRONIC ORGANIZATION

ELECTRONIC DOCUMENTS

	1	2	3
I have a logical system of folders on my computer for electronic documents.	✔	✔	✔

1. Not really

2. To some extent

3. To a great extent

I use a manageable number of folders on my computer for filing.

1. Not really

2. Somewhat

3. Yes

I file my electronic documents.

1. Rarely, if ever

2. Some of the time

3. Most of the time

When I retrieve documents, I find what I look for:

1. With great difficulty

2. Somewhat easily

3. Very easily

I back up my computer system.

1. Not really

2. Locally to an external drive, thumb drive, or computer

3. Both locally and to a backup server system or service

Tally the check marks in the 1, 2, and 3 columns.

EMAIL	1 ✔	2 ✔	3 ✔

I check my email:

1. 24/7, all incoming as it arrives while I'm awake
2. Quite frequently, whenever I want to take a work break
3. Only occasionally at specific times of the day

I use a system to review and respond to email.

1. Not really, email stays in my inbox until I'm over quota
2. Somewhat, I read and file email when I have time
3. Yes, I have a way to quickly handle incoming email

I have a thought-out system of folders for filing email.

1. I don't really use folders
2. Somewhat, I add a new folder as I need one
3. Yes, it corresponds to my business needs

I use automatic electronic methods for handling email.

1. Not at all, I want to check each email as it comes in
2. Somewhat, I have a folder for newsletters
3. Yes, I have defined rules that automatically sort email

I print my email.

1. Yes, I review my email in printed form
2. Most of the mail that contains information I might need
3. Occasionally, for an immediate need of a physical copy

When I search for emails, I find what I am looking for:

1. With great difficulty
2. Somewhat easily
3. Very easily

Tally the check marks in the 1, 2, and 3 columns.

LEVEL 3: TIME MANAGEMENT

	1 ✔	2 ✔	3 ✔

CALENDAR

I write down my appointments.

1. On sticky notes or other paper notes
2. On several different calendars
3. On only one calendar

I remind myself of an upcoming appointment:

1. With sticky notes
2. By checking my calendar frequently throughout the day
3. With an electronic reminder or automatic alarm

I am knowledgeable about electronic calendar capabilities (recurring appointments, coding, labels).

1. Not at all
2. Somewhat
3. To a great extent

I have explored different calendar systems.

1. Not at all
2. Somewhat
3. To a great extent

TASK LIST

I review my daily plans.

1. Rarely, if ever
2. On days I have time, usually weekly
3. At a specific time each day

I list my tasks and activities.

1. On random notes to myself
2. On a to-do list that I update
3. On my calendar, with the time needed to complete time

	1	2	3
My day follows my plan.	✔	✔	✔

My day follows my plan.

1. Rarely, if ever
2. Somewhat
3. Most of the time

My day is disrupted by staff or other people calling, text messaging, or walking into my office.

1. Frequently
2. Occasionally
3. Rarely

I spend time during my workday checking Facebook, doing online shopping, or handling similar distraction.

1. Frequently
2. Occasionally
3. Rarely, if ever

I break down projects into manageable tasks.

1. Rarely, if ever
2. Occasionally
3. Frequently

Tally the check marks in the 1, 2, and 3 columns.

LEVEL 4: ACTIVITY-GOAL ALIGNMENT

I establish goals for my business.

1. Rarely, if ever
2. Sometimes
3. Frequently

I review the goals for my business.

1. Rarely, if ever
2. Once or twice a year
3. Monthly or more frequently

LEVEL 4: ACTIVITY-GOAL ALIGNMENT (CONT.)	1 ✔	2 ✔	3 ✔

I establish goals for the other areas of my life.

1. No, I do not create personal goals

2. I look at some personal goals

3. Yes, I create a plan with life goals

I break down goals into activities to accomplish goals.

1. Rarely, if ever

2. To a moderate extent

3. To a great extent

I hold meetings with my staff, customers, or others to align business goals with needs identified.

1. Rarely, if ever

2. Sometimes

3. Frequently

I communicate company goals to my staff.

1. Rarely, if ever

2. Sometimes by email or a similar method

3. Frequently, by phone, by email, and in-person meetings

Tally the check marks in the 1, 2, and 3 columns.

**TABLE 2-2. TALLY YOUR PRODUCTIVITY
PYRAMID ASSESSMENT SCORES**

TALLY OF CHECK MARKS BY COLUMN	1 ✔	2 ✔	3 ✔	Mostly 1, 2, 3
LEVEL 1: PHYSICAL ORGANIZATION				
LEVEL 2: ELECTRONIC ORGANIZATION				
LEVEL 3: TIME MANAGEMENT				
LEVEL 4: ACTIVITY-GOAL ALIGNMENT				

Level 1: Physical Organization

If your tally shows you marked mostly 1s, you could benefit from the chapter on managing your physical clutter. What you are doing, or not doing, to organize your paper files probably isn't working for you. You will want to consider new approaches, knowing that there is no one right way, just the way that works best for you. This is the area you will want to tackle first in the book.

If you marked mostly 2s, then you will also benefit by reviewing the chapter on managing physical clutter to see if there are some changes you could make to improve your productivity. Remember the Peak Productivity Pyramid. This might be the best place to start unless there is another area you are more anxious to start right now.

If you marked mostly 3s, then you probably have achieved or are close to achieving physical organization, but you could, perhaps, pick up a tip or two by skimming the chapter on this topic. You can skip this area for now, come back to it later, if you wish, and tackle an area where you can see greater productivity returns.

It is rare to find people who like to organize and file papers (unless, perhaps, they're using it as an excuse to procrastinate some other, more onerous task). Even professional organizers who sort, file, and declutter for a living rarely enjoy the process of filing. Personally, I have never met *anyone* who enjoys the task, myself included.

For most people, the satisfaction usually comes in terms of the ease of retrieving something when needed, having more pleasant surroundings to work in, and the overall increase in productivity. So don't be too hard on yourself if you've identified this as an area of improvement—you're not alone! As you will discover in the chapter on physical organization, there are many different strategies that can make it easier for you to create a more productive environment.

Level 2: Electronic Organization

If you marked mostly 1s, you could benefit from the chapter on improving your electronic organization. What you are doing, or not doing, isn't working for you. You should look at new ways to manage your electronic files more productively. You should consider clearing up your physical clutter first, though, if that is also an area where you need improvement.

If you marked mostly 2s, then you will benefit by reviewing the chapter on electronic organization to see if there are some changes you could make or new ideas to consider for improving your electronic productivity. You might want to hone these skills before moving on to the more advanced skills of time management and activity-goal alignment.

If you marked mostly 3s, then you probably have achieved or are close to achieving electronic organization. Even so, you could find some additional ways to make handling electronic files easier if you at least skim the chapter. You can always come back to this material if you prefer to tackle a section with greater return first.

We have been living with e-mail systems for two decades, yet even now, after all these years, our educational institutions still don't teach e-mail management strategies. It is usually the same in the workforce. No one says to us on our first day in a new job, "Here are the subfolders you will want to set up, and you should plan to check your e-mail only four times a day." Instead, we are left to figure it out as we go. Sometimes we get stuck with decisions we made along the way from that first day we started working in a job on a new computer. Then, as we get bombarded with more and more e-mail and greater volumes of electronic documents to file, we're always trying to catch up, but still using the inadequate system that we started with.

When e-mail and texting are your primary means of communication, growing and maintaining a system can be even more challenging. Often, you don't feel that it is possible to be away from it.

Karen works in the mortgage lending office of a large local bank. She has a lot of daily interruptions with requests for information, meetings, client negotiations, and so on. Her favorite way to communicate in this fast-paced environment with her assistant Donna is through e-mail. But Donna has to sit outside Karen's office glued to her computer, incessantly checking incoming messages. If her boss wants anything, anytime, Donna needs to respond immediately; that's her job. In the chapter on electronic organization you will learn about taking back control of your e-mail so that it isn't taking control of you; you'll also learn how to better manage your electronic documents so that you can retrieve them when you need them.

Level 3: Time Management

If you marked mostly 1s, you could benefit from the chapter on time management. What you are doing, or not doing, to manage your calendar and task list isn't working for you. If you have improvements to make in the areas of physical clutter and managing electronic clutter, then work on those areas first.

If you marked mostly 2s, then you will also benefit by reviewing the chapter on time management to see if there are some changes you could make to improve your productivity. Likewise, if you feel that you can also improve your physical and electronic clutter, it is beneficial to be proficient in those areas first.

If you marked mostly 3s, then you probably have achieved proficiency on time management but could pick up a tip or two by at least skimming the chapter. You will probably want to start in another area where you can derive the greatest benefit.

When asked, some people immediately assess themselves as being poor time managers. If the assessment shows that you can benefit from learning more about time management, or if you believe this is an area that needs improvement, then it is important to first understand that you cannot manage time. Time is what is on the clock, and you can't add or subtract it. We all operate with the same amount of time in a day: twenty-four hours. We can only manage our behavior around time and what we choose to do with the time we have. Time management is about choice.

Some people think of time management as delegating. To others it is scheduling tasks, and to others it's the feeling of never getting enough done in a day. Time management is really choice management. Of all the choices you are managing at this minute, which one are you going to choose to do? Understanding that you have control over that choice is time management. It is about what you choose to do with your time in a given day. With all the options you have for a given day, which ones are you going to pick? The chapter on time management will show you how to manage your behavior around time and how you can feel better about how you use the time you have.

Level 4: Activity-Goal Alignment

If you marked mostly 1s, you could benefit from the chapter on alignment of your activities to your goals. Having a clear sense of what you want to accomplish in both your business and your life will give you a greater sense of accomplishment and improve the likelihood that you will achieve what you want.

If you marked mostly 2s, then you will benefit by reviewing the chapter to see if there are some changes you could make or new ideas you should consider to improve your practices around activity-goal alignment. You might want to hone these skills before moving on to the more advanced topic of possibilities.

If you marked mostly 3s, then you probably have achieved or are close to achieving activity-goal alignment. You are aligning the tasks you perform every day with the goals you have set out to accomplish. You should find some additional ways to improve your activity-goal alignment if you at least skim the chapter. You can always come back to this section if you prefer to tackle an area with greater return first. However, if you have arrived at this point and your assessment shows that you are accomplished in all four areas—physical organization, electronic organization, task management, and activity-goal alignment—then start at the beginning and read through the four areas quickly before tackling the chapter on possibility.

It's hard to believe, but some entrepreneurs and executives don't have a business plan at all and simply operate to meet the day-to-day needs of the business. Most of the people who do not have goals usually have not set aside time to think about what they want their future to look like. Even when people have a business plan with goals, they can be so business focused that they forget to think about goals for the other areas of their lives. Others may have developed goals, but they revisit them so infrequently that they remain as goals, the big plan way out there on the horizon, never getting any closer, even with the continuing passage of time.

If your assessment points to the need for more work around aligning your daily activities to your goals, then the chapter on activity-goal alignment will help you recognize the ways that you can become more productive in the long-term achievement of your goals by more purposefully breaking down your goals into achievable tasks.

Where people often get stuck is when they haven't set aside time to think about their goals, or they have the goals and haven't figured out how to make them happen because of the everyday busyness in their lives. They haven't figured out how to break the big goal into tasks they can work on every day.

The other way to think about time management and activity-goal alignment is as life management. Time is life, and it's your life. You might be thinking that this book will help you achieve all your goals at work, but if you want to enter the realm of possibility, it can't just be about work. You have to consider all aspects of your life and your productivity holistically.

Level 5: Possibility

You might be wondering why there isn't an assessment for level 5 of the Peak Productivity Pyramid. It's because possibility is not a place you arrive at and then say, "Yeah, I'm here! I made it!" Possibility, like Maslow's self-actualization, is where you are constantly assessing, reassessing, and moving your target goals; it's where you continue to explore how to best use the time you have. In order to increase your productivity, what can you do now that you could not have done before? What are the possibilities that lie before you? The chapter on possibility will help you explore what is possible for you. You will want to feel proficient in the other areas before tackling this chapter.

The first step in the Peak Productivity Pyramid System is determining which level of the pyramid is the best place for you to start your journey. Taking the Peak Productivity Pyramid Assessment, or working with a productivity consultant who can lead you through an assessment, will save you time and increase the likelihood of your success in mastering each of the other four levels before tackling level 5, possibility.

Once you know which level is the best place for you to start, you can jump directly to that chapter and focus on what you want to improve. On the other hand, reading through all the preceding levels could give you new insights as well, because as you have learned, you will never complete any level. There will always be innovations and new approaches and techniques. You never know what new skills you might pick up at each of the levels.

PRODUCTIVITY POINTERS

- Taking the assessment provided in this chapter, or working with a consultant who can lead you through the questions, will help you to clarify why improving your productivity is important and where you should start on your journey to improve your skills.
- Once you identify areas that need improvement the most, you can start there, knowing you can always revisit the previous levels.
- To achieve the fifth level of the Peak Productivity Pyramid—possibility, or fulfilling your potential—you will need to achieve sufficient proficiency at all the previous levels.

CHAPTER 3

LEVEL 1: PHYSICAL ORGANIZATION

K nowing that I am a Certified Professional Organizer® (CPO), people often ask me, "Have you always been organized?"

The truth is, not always, and my mother is the one who reminded me of this fact. There was a time when keeping my closet clean was particularly challenging for me. As a fourteen-year-old, my social life was important, and on this particular occasion, my friends and I made plans to go to the movies on a Friday night. All week my mother reminded me that my closet had to be straightened out before I could go to the movies. All my clothes had to be folded, hung, or otherwise put away. I kept putting it off; I just couldn't face the mess.

When Friday evening arrived, my closet was still in a tangle of clothes, and I was grounded; no movie for me. Instead of going to the movies with my friends, I spent the evening sulking in my room and organizing my closet.

At some point, as I was wrangling a pile of sweaters into the bottom drawer in my closet, it hit me. The reason I wasn't putting my clothes away is because the closet system wasn't working for me. I hated putting my things back in the drawers where I couldn't see exactly what I had. What a waste of time it was taking that extra step of opening and closing drawers. I am a visual person, so being able to see things is important to me.

After I finished putting everything away, I said to my mother, "If I'm going to be able to keep my closet organized, I need a new system, one with shelves instead of drawers." She agreed, and the two of us began sketching out concepts of closet storage that would work well for me. With a little help from a handyman, my dream closet became a reality. I was so excited! From that day on, my closet has always been organized.

What I've learned about organizing is that often people are trying to fit their clutter into systems that aren't working for them. They try to stuff everything into a system that doesn't fit the way they can deal with things or retrieve them; as a consequence, the task of getting organized seems insurmountable. There are entire books on filing techniques; many businesses are organized around filing systems. But rather than cover all the possible systems, this chapter has a different purpose. The two primary purposes of this chapter are to help you:

1. Tackle the initial problem of physical clutter in a way that helps you get it under control as quickly and as easily as possible.
2. Evaluate and determine what systems will work best for you, even if that means thinking outside the filing cabinet.

Even if clutter isn't a problem for you, you might find new ways of organizing that will streamline your access and reduce your filing time.

WHY CLEARING THE CLUTTER MATTERS

Clutter is the most common reason people first contact me. Physical organization is the first step in the Peak Productivity Pyramid System, and

I have learned that no matter what else is keeping people from reaching their goals and being effective and productive, without first clearing the physical disorganization, every other step in the Peak Productivity Pyramid System falls by the wayside. As Maslow would attest, it is hard to think about love when you're starving and cold. People who have an office that is cluttered are more likely to feel stressed each time they walk into their office. According to the National Association of Professional Organizers (NAPO), the average American spends one year of his or her life looking for lost or misplaced items.

In addition to increasing our efficiency, there are other reasons why achieving physical organization is important. According to a 2011 study by CareerBuilder, 28 percent of employers say they are less likely to promote someone who has a disorganized desk.[1] Nearly two in five employers say that a cluttered desk negatively impacts their perception of that person.

Presenting an organized workspace has a positive effect not only on your ability to get things done more efficiently, but also on how people judge your performance. When it comes to what they wear to work, to an interview, to a meeting, most people "get it." They will dress for success, wearing what's appropriate for the occasion, knowing the importance of first impressions. Dressing your office to create a positive impression has the same positive effect, and a messy office will make a poor impression.

Think about how much paper comes into your life every day, between everything you get in the mail, the kids' school papers, and other personal papers at home. Then at work you receive notes, memos, faxes, and other documentation. We are bombarded with paper. For most of us, this paper tends to accumulate in stacks, and the stacks grow faster than we can keep up with it. Here is the system I have found that works best for dealing with issue one—what to do when you feel overwhelmed by the clutter.

GETTING RID OF CLUTTER

Everyone knows intuitively that getting rid of clutter is important; however, we are still challenged by the vast amounts of paper we receive. The first three goals in achieving physical organization are simple:

1. Get rid of as much paper as you can, so you minimize your space needs.
2. Store what you save efficiently, so you can find what you need.
3. Set up a system for handling your papers as they come in.

It takes time to get organized, and because we don't have enough time, we often postpone it. But if you think about it, your time spent organizing is an investment. You are investing time to get organized because ultimately it is going to save you time. To become more productive and more effective at managing your time, you have to start at the first level of the pyramid: physical organization. You need to start by creating a paper organization system that's going to work for you. It's far more efficient to keep your paper organized and therefore avoid clutter in the first place than it is to let the paper pile up and deal with it later.

There is a simple way to handle all the papers that continually come into your life. This system for managing your papers is about learning to make decisions.

According to organizational expert Barbara Hemphill, one way to define clutter is to think about it as delayed decisions. When you fail to make a decision each time you handle a piece of paper, it becomes clutter. Stacks of accumulated paper are a result of delaying to decide what to do with each paper as it arrives. Every piece of paper that comes into your life falls into one of three categories:

1. You're going to shred or recycle the paper.
2. It's a document that requires some type of action, such as a bill to pay, an RSVP to mail, or a form to fill out.
3. It's something that you have to keep, either for legal reasons or because you might need to refer to it.

These are the "Three To's" of sorting for all papers: to do, to keep, or to toss. When you use the Three To's of sorting, then you can make decisions quickly for all your papers by placing them into one of just three categories.

Here's how you apply this method to achieve physical organization. Imagine you have piles of paper spread around on your desk or on the floor. The first thing to do is to gather all the papers together and then sort them into the three categories by physically creating three piles.

1. *To Toss.* These are all the papers that you no longer need or that you can access elsewhere. Papers on your "to toss" pile either get recycled or shredded.
2. *To Do.* Create a second pile for all the papers that require you to take some action. If you need to schedule a meeting with somebody, respond to an invitation, pay your bill, put those papers together in one "to do" pile.
3. *To Keep.* Everything that you need to save but you don't need to do anything with—a bank statement, papers regarding medical history, tax receipts, or other items that you need to refer to in the future—place in another pile called "to keep."

The mistake most people make when they first tackle the task of organizing their stacks of papers is that instead of starting with three simple piles, they immediately try to sort everything into many different subcategories, such as financial, medical, and projects. When they tackle sorting that way, it takes much longer and can feel overwhelming.

Using the Three To's of sorting is similar to creating a big-picture view of your clutter; it's a way of doing top-level sorting. When you first sort into three piles, the goal is really to get rid of as much paper as you can. These days it's easy to retrieve information online. If an item is a manual or something that you can go online and find, you can make the decision to toss it. If you know something is available elsewhere, get rid of it. If you have expired receipts or coupons, it's okay to let go and get rid of them right away. You won't have to make a decision about that piece of paper again later. Once you sort all your papers into these three stacks, you will be ready to file the piles.

To Toss

The first of your three piles to tackle will clear more space and immediately reduce the clutter. Throwing paper away is the easiest way to declutter, and yet many people find it difficult to let go of something they think they might need. As you hesitate, think of where else you might be able to retrieve this information if you were to need it someday. Is it really gone forever, or are there other sources to get it from? Remember, the papers you are handling now that you don't throw away are going to take up valuable space. You might end up handling them again and again as you clean out overstuffed folders and cabinets.

In this day of privacy requirements and the threat of identity theft, it is important to shred any sensitive documents before you throw them out. Then you can toss the remaining papers into your recycling bin. Make it easy for yourself and other people in your workplace to recycle by having separate trash and recycle bins. Once you've cleared some space by throwing out what you don't need, then you're ready for the "to do" pile.

To Do

Clutter created by this category, in particular, is more a result of a weakness in time management practices than poor organizational skills. Eventually your to-do papers will tie into your time management system, but at this point you are just going to put them into a single "to do" stack. You are not going to stop and take action on each paper as you sort. To start, you will need a simple vertical filing system, stackers on the desk, smart folders, or any kind of system that works for you to keep track of your to-do papers.

With your "to toss" and "to do" papers out of the way, you are ready for the "to keep" pile.

To Keep

Nearly everyone uses filing cabinets to store their files because filing cabinets have been an effective way of storing paper for as long as we can remember. Usually, you'll have filing cabinets on either one or both sides of your desk, where you file papers that you are currently working on or need to access frequently. In addition, there are usually one or more larger filing cabinets farther away that may require you to step away from your desk to access. Those are good for the papers that you don't need to access frequently, but that you still need to retain.

If you are using a filing cabinet, you need the following supplies:

* Hanging folders
* Labels
* File folders

Now you are ready to file those papers you need to keep. You will sort them into subcategories, such as financial, medical, and whatever makes sense to you for your life and your papers. Which system of filing and retrieving will work best for you? Here are some of the primary systems people use exclusively or in combination with other systems:

- Alphabetical
- Categorical
- Chronological
- Numerical
- Address

Let's take a more detailed look at the two filing systems used most broadly: alphabetical and categorical.

- *Alphabetical.* Alphabetical filing is usually easy to set up and to delegate; anyone can set it up and maintain it for you. Set up hanging files labeled A through Z. Then file your folders alphabetically, either by the person's last name, company name, or however the file is labeled by subject. You can place a client folder in the hanging file for letter A, and if the client's last name is Austin, you put that file right before the file labeled Auto Repair. It doesn't matter that it's a hodgepodge of categories because everything is alphabetical. It's easy to retrieve for people who remember things by their names or subject. It's easy to set up, it's easy to keep up, it's easy for delegation, so it's very widely used.

  If you use the alphabetical system you may, however, want to have two separate alphabetical cabinets: one for personal and one for business files. In fact, I advise that you should always keep business and personal papers separate, especially if you are claiming the office on your taxes. If you get audited, the IRS will want to see separation of business and personal paperwork.
- *Categorical.* Another option is to create hanging files in different parts of the file drawers based on category. You might have a cat-

egory for clients, a category for presentations, a category for accounting, a category for research; choose whatever categories make sense for your business. Within the categories, you can (but don't have to) alphabetize. It doesn't really matter because usually a category won't be so big that you need to subcategorize. However, for businesses that have many clients, usually they'll file categorically, then alphabetically within the category.

When you are filing into a cabinet, it is most important to label your files so that you can retrieve and reference information easily. People often struggle with which labels to use for their files and what to call them. The truth is there is no right and wrong way; it's a personal decision that is up to you. Name your files according to what will come to your mind when you go to retrieve that information. Call each file whatever makes sense to you.

APRIL'S STORY

Several years ago, I walked into the home of a residential business owner in North Providence, Rhode Island. Rather than having a single room dedicated for her office, she shared her office space with a number of different rooms. She must have had thirty piles all over her dining room floor, dining room table, and family room floor. Some of the piles had one paper; others were bigger. You could see she had started to file, because on top of each pile there was a sticky note labeling the pile. She was trying to add papers to the piles, yet it was taking her forever to find the right pile—"Where is my medical information 2011 pile?"—for each paper.

I started by teaching her to sort using just three piles: to do, to keep, and to toss. I illustrated the importance of keeping it simple. She didn't need an elaborate filing system to accommodate diverse needs; she just needed a way to catch up with a filing system that was out of control. Look at the before situation in Figure 3-1 and after picture in Figure 3-2. What a difference!

Figure 3-1. Dining room physical clutter before. *Author's photo.*

Figure 3-2. Dining room physical clutter after. *Author's photo.*

It was later, when we were working on her "to keep" pile, that April confessed the reason she had never filed her papers was because she didn't know what to call the individual folders. She had even gone so far as to look up on the Internet the right names, as if she needed permission from the filing police. She was afraid she would label them incorrectly. All the while, she wasn't filing because she was afraid of calling a file the wrong name.

"April, you can call them anything you like. They are your folders. Just figure out something you will remember and go with it," I told her.

She was visibly astounded. "I can? I can just pick any name I want?" I then helped her make up the names, and I remember how we laughed as she came up with a silly name she put on a folder for her kids. "I can call it that?" she said. "I can make up a label like that, really?"

I nodded. "Yes, you can, because it's your system; you own these filing cabinets. You can do whatever you want."

It is common for people not to know how to label files. But you are the best person to decide because you have a better chance of remembering something that has meaning to you.

One mistake many people make when they name folders is having one called "miscellaneous." Rather than using a name that describes what is in the folder, even if it's silly, they call it miscellaneous. In six months, they forget what is in the folder. Often it becomes a catchall folder with mixed content. It's like another pile, just in a folder. Even if it sounds silly, use a label that clearly describes what is in the folder.

While this was an extreme example, I have encountered many businesspeople who are stuck because of a simple hang-up. Before we continue to explore the details of sorting and achieving physical organization, let's step back for a moment and remind ourselves of the Peak Productivity Pyramid. Recall, we are on level 1, physical organization, and a key theme of the Peak Productivity Pyramid System is that it operates like Maslow's hierarchy of personal needs—it is difficult to pursue the next level until the current level is achieved. Look back at Figure 3-1 and imagine that workspace belongs to someone who is managing a successful business. Does that office look like the workspace of someone who can effectively manage her time and align her activities to her goals? It becomes impossible if you are constantly drowning in paperwork.

USING THE THREE TO'S OF SORTING

Once you establish a filing system to sort and file the pile you need to keep, you are ready to deal with all the papers that come in daily. Every day you get mail, take papers out to work on a project, print an e-mail to take to a meeting. Then there are the papers people drop off for your inbox, such as memos or papers you need to sign. If you sort these papers daily into your three categories of to do, to keep, and to toss, it usually takes about five minutes. If you only do it once a week, it will take you at least forty-five minutes because you have to think back and try to remember the circumstances, then make the decision. It is much easier and more efficient if you process your paperwork daily as it comes in. After all, it is much easier to find five minutes in your day than forty-five.

Processing is simply sorting into your three categories. Then, if you want, you can sort the "to keep" papers right away or put them in a file, some kind of a box, for filing into your cabinets later.

FILING OPTIONS

Now that you understand the Three To's of sorting and how to use it for staying ahead of your clutter, let's look at the different options of filing. While most people use filing cabinets, some people have a lot of resistance to them, either because they don't like to have to open the drawer, find the folder, then stick something in it, or because they want something that's a little faster or more visual. For others, it's just because they never really learned how to file properly.

The good news is that we have lots of options for different filing methods that we can use. It's nice to think outside the filing cabinet. There are desktop filing boxes (see Figure 3-3 and Figure 3-4), which are great, especially for teenagers who love to have a small filing box to hide their papers away. You can also use hanging folders right on the desk for current papers or papers that you need to retrieve throughout the year.

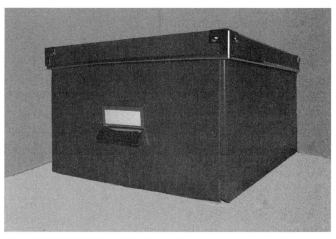

Figure 3-3. Closed desktop filing box. *Author's photo.*

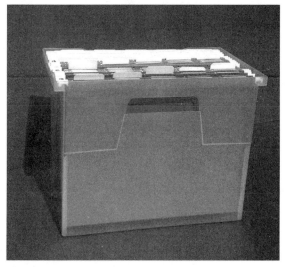

Figure 3-4. Open desktop filing box. *Author's photo.*

Many businesspeople have used a variety of desktop systems. Some people have boxes for different categories and have a box per category right on their desk, and it looks pretty. The benefit of filing boxes is that they are mobile, so they work especially well if you are on the road a lot.

Decorative boxes (see Figure 3-5) are another option. Some people like the look of pretty, decorative boxes, especially if they work from home. There are so many options available. Just as with file cabinets, you can be creative and decide how you want to organize and label your boxes.

If you don't like to file in folders at all, you can also think about using magazine holders (see Figure 3-6) stacked up on a shelf, right in front of you. If your desk faces a wall, you can put up a couple of shelves for magazine holders. Label one magazine holder per category and you can just throw the paper in there, right in the envelope. You don't even have to take it out of the envelope if you don't want to.

There are a lot of different methods that don't involve hanging files and manila folders. Find what works for you and then stick to it and

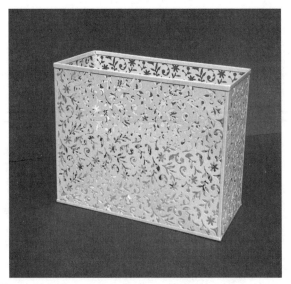

Figure 3-5. Decorative desktop filing box. *Author's photo.*

Figure 3-6. Magazine holders. *Author's photo.*

make the commitment to always stay on top of the incoming papers with the Three To's of sorting: to do, to keep, to toss.

ADAM'S STORY

Adam is a Realtor, but he also owns a number of residential rental properties from which he generates a nice side income. He wasn't doing any filing at all; he didn't even take things out of envelopes. He just knew where things were and kept these envelopes rubber-banded together. His home office was a mess. His wife pleaded with him to come up with an organizational system. But he was adamant that he was not going to file. He hated filing, and there was no talking, no trying to tweak systems, nothing she could do to convince him. The solution we found was using magazine holders.

We put up shelves on the wall and we labeled each magazine holder with the property address. As mail came in, he threw the envelopes into the respective property box. He didn't have to open the envelopes; he didn't have to do anything. It was great because it mirrored his current system with the rubber-banded envelopes by address. Then we created rules around the system that worked for him. When a box was full, he was not allowed to create piles around the box. He could either archive the box or add a new one, depending on the situation. He was happy; his wife was happy; it was a good solution.

If a system isn't working for you, you might need to get inventive to find one that does work.

MORE ON FILING

When working with people who have issues dealing with physical clutter, I usually start by asking, "Why is this system not working for you? Why are the piles here?"

Usually they say, "I hate to file. I've always hated it."

So I ask, "Why do you hate it?"

What most people have taught me is that one of the main reasons they don't file is because the filing cabinet is not easily accessible. They especially find it frustrating to access the filing cabinet that contains their current projects with the papers they need every day. Those should be within arm's reach.

Ideally, you need at least one small filing drawer on or near your desk, so you can put all your current papers there. When you are sitting at your desk and you are processing papers, you should be able to file and retrieve your essential papers right there, without having to get up and go to the filing cabinet. If you don't have a desk with a filing cabinet, buy a rolling filing drawer that you can put right next to your desk. It doesn't have to be expensive; it just needs to be functional. Proximity is the biggest reason people don't file their papers. Just changing that and creating easier access will make it more likely that you will file the papers as you use them.

Another reason people resist filing is because they have inherited a system. The CFO of a law firm had been hired to replace the retiring CFO. Shortly after starting, his office was a disaster, and it was hindering his ability to jump into a high-paced job. What we found is that the filing system he had inherited wasn't working for him because he was used to filing alphabetically and not color-coding by category. He had preferred binders, but the previous CFO had a completely different system that he was trying to adapt to.

We tweaked the system by mirroring the past alphabetical system that had worked well for him. We worked with the way he liked to access information, instead of trying to make him adapt to a system that, even though technically correct, wasn't working for him.

So, first look at your current system and think about why it is not working. If it's a proximity issue, or an inherited system issue, those are easy to fix.

Another issue can be an overstuffed cabinet. People resist filing when it's a physical struggle to get things into the cabinet where nothing fits anymore. The solution is simply scheduling time to go through the old files. Toss obsolete files and create an archive system for those files you need to keep. Take the old files out of the filing system that you're using currently in your office and put them in bankers' boxes. Label them, then archive them in a separate location. If you don't need to retrieve them often, you can store them in a basement, attic, or off-site storage area. Archiving will make room in the existing cabinet drawer for the files to move in and out easily.

If none of these solutions are working or if you absolutely hate the idea of filing inside a cabinet drawer, then you might need to explore further alternatives. A lot of people, especially creative people, like to have things that are visually accessible to them. They like to see something, either for a memory trigger or to get inspired.

You're in luck. There are still alternatives that can help. So if you're a visual person and you like stylish or pretty things, you can buy decorative filing boxes that complement your office decor. Label the boxes so that it's easy for you to throw things inside. Then create the filing rules for your system. For example, once the box is full you have to either archive or throw out things, except for what you need to keep for taxes, financial reasons, or further reference. You simply create rules around your made-up new filing system.

JOHN'S STORY

The first time I walked into John's office, there was one little pile of papers on his desk. These are the papers he uses in his day's work. He is very comfortable with this small stack because he knows exactly what's there. He has no trouble retrieving papers. One day I was asking him about projects. "How do you keep track of your big projects?" He walked me toward a back office that was always locked. When he opened the door, I was shocked. He was always so organized, but there, behind this door, it looked like his personal dumping ground. This back office was evidence of his lack of a system for some of his bigger, personal projects.

He tried to justify it by saying, "I know everything is there." But for him, it was really overwhelming, and not enough was getting done. So we agreed that he would have to spend time in the back office at least once a week to tackle some of these projects.

A couple of months later, I asked him what he had accomplished. He hadn't gone in once. He was overwhelmed; that room was a black hole for him. On one level, having that back office worked for him, because when he put papers there, then his active papers and his current office were completely under control. These other tasks weren't urgent but still fairly important and needed attention, but he wasn't moving forward with any of them. When we started talking about what those piles were, we discovered that they fell into three broad categories:

1. *Things He Could Let Go.* Nothing adverse would happen if he did not take action.

2. *Tasks That Needed Attention.* He could incorporate them into his current time management system; he just wasn't doing it yet.

3. *Reading Material.* There were files he wanted to read for his own edification.

We incorporated a lot of the projects that were piled up there, in the back room, into his calendar and incorporated the papers related to them into his current filing system. When the calendar prompted him to work on a project, the papers were accessible. For the papers he wanted to read, we created a traveling system. He could carry with him reading materials for those times when he was waiting—for example, when he was holding an open house and waiting for buyers to show up. The remaining papers were filed or tossed. He still has a back room, only now he regularly tackles any project he keeps there because he has a system to manage it.

ADVANCED TECHNIQUES

Here is an introduction to some other systems that are more complex than the most common ones, but for some people, these techniques are the most effective.

- *The Tickler System.* The tickler system, also known as the 43 folders method, is a way to keep track of your to-do papers. While it can be overly complicated for some people, for others it is their preferred way. Create a series of folders numbered 1 through 31, for the days of the month, then one folder for each of the months of the year labeled January through December. If you have an action item scheduled for a month or so away—say, February 1 of next year—you throw it into the February folder. You know it will be there when you need it. When February rolls around, you sort the papers into the daily folders labeled 1 through 31, deciding what tasks you will work on each day. When you pull out the February files at the beginning of that month, you look in folder 1 and take care of the tasks you've allocated for that day. The next day you get the number 2 folder, and you take care of those tasks.

As you are completing those tasks, you'll be getting papers for March and April, so you drop them into the monthly folders. And then when March comes, you put any tasks or to-dos that are left from February into a future file, passing them along to March or April, for example, or else you decide you do not need to do them at all. As you can see, it is quite a specialized system, and very few people find using this system effective.

One client of mine who uses this system has her administrative assistant maintain the tickler for her. She takes the papers out each month, puts them in the day folders, and places incoming tasks into the appropriate folders. The client spends none of her time handling her tickler system and only touches it when undertaking the current day's papers and working on the tasks. This system will work best for someone who has the ability to delegate the maintenance of it.

- *Color Coding.* Within categories a lot of people like to color-code. They use green folders for financial files, red folders for medical, blue folders for clients, and yellow folders for research, for example. Color coding works well for people who are visual and creative. For some people it doesn't matter. If it doesn't matter for you, personally, I advise against it for the simple reason that it makes filing more complicated. You always need to have enough supplies on hand for the different colors. If, say, you need to run to the store or order supplies online, it will add an extra step or stop you from filing. Let's say that you are color-coding by category and you get new financial papers, and you need to create a new folder for them. You go to your supplies and find that you are out of green folders. Now you can't file because you don't have green folders. Unless you find color coding an essential component that helps you with filing and retrieving, I suggest keeping the system as simple as possible.

- *Premade Filing Systems.* There are also many premade filing systems available. There are even professional organizers who are certified in implementing various systems. But before signing up, think long and hard about how the system fits with your needs, whether it is simple enough, or whether you can delegate filing easily to someone else.

- *Magazine Clutter.* People typically keep magazines for articles they want to read at some time in the future. Create a system for managing your magazines by clipping the articles you want to read to carry with you (like John did, when he realized he could catch up on reading during those times when he was waiting for buyers to show up at an open house). If you have other reasons for keeping them, then you need to establish rules—for example, discard any journals at year's end that are one year old or more. Most information today is found online, so before you keep a journal that you think you might need to reference someday, check to see if you have easy access to the same information online. (See the chapter on electronic organization for more recommendations.)

- *Books, Binders, and More.* These kinds of physical elements require adequate storage. Keeping your space free of clutter can only be accomplished when you have the space you need to accommodate what you have. Either put up a shelf or buy bookshelves if you have space. There isn't any magic formula. You can only keep what you have room for.

GRACE'S STORY

Grace loved The Container Store. She shopped there often and knew about all their products, even the latest ones. Meanwhile, her office was so piled up with papers that you couldn't even open the door more than a thirty-degree crack, just to scooch by. There were papers everywhere. She was obsessed with knowing about all the container systems available, but she was paralyzed by not knowing how to process the papers. She knew how to file; she had reviewed all the systems available and had learned everything about the system she wanted. But she didn't apply it to the papers surrounding her office because she was so overwhelmed.

We talked about the Three To's of sorting and started creating piles. Even after six months of biting away at this huge undertaking, all the progress we made was not very noticeable. It is not about the organizing system as much as having a reliable process in place. If you are starting with an office steeped in clutter (as Grace was), the more elaborate the system you're setting up, the more difficult it is to organize.

Premade systems are often the biggest time-saver when you are starting from scratch without an inherited system or too much existing clutter. Many of these premade systems are easy to set up. However, even if setup is easy, sticking to it is the most difficult part. The simplicity of the Three To's system of sorting is time-tested, and it is the best course to organize and maintain your papers, even when using another system as well.

MARGARET'S STORY

Margaret is a self-employed human resource (HR) consultant who runs her business out of her home office. She had previously worked with another professional organizer who, as she put it, "Just wasn't my style."

So she gave up, which led to more and more piles accumulating everywhere.

My first visit revealed a bedroom that was converted into a home office (see Figure 3-7). It was a small room. She had an L-shaped desk with a small bookshelf next to it. She had a two-drawer filing cabinet behind her desk. She had a filing drawer on her desk. The bedroom closet had been converted into office storage with shelves for office supplies and a wide filing cabinet inside. She had a lot of filing space.

Yet she had piles of papers all over her desk and all over the floor and all around the perimeter of the room. There were lots of papers to be dealt with. We looked at the methods for filing she had in place, and there were a couple of different ones. She had the files in cabinet drawers, but she also had binders that she used for information that was related to HR laws and regulations, which change every year. It was clear that she also needed better systems to separate business and personal papers, because she had medical records on her desk piled next to her client papers.

We worked together using the Three To's of sorting method. It took us approximately sixteen hours just to sort all the papers into piles to do,

Figure 3-7. Small office before. *Author's photo.*

to keep, and to toss. (Sorting is usually a pretty quick process, so this many hours gives you an idea of the magnitude of her problem.) Once we finished sorting, her action pile was big because she had not tackled her papers in a long time. Even though having a large action pile might seem overwhelming, having the stack organized gave her a starting point and made the task seem more manageable.

Next, we looked at her HR binder system, which was working quite well for her. Because she liked it so much, we used the binder system for some other categories of papers, too. For example, we created binders for each client instead of having several folders of information tucked away in drawers.

For each client we dedicated a three-ring binder, labeled the spine with the client's name, and filed all the binders alphabetically on the shelf in her office. When she visited a client, she had a professional binder she could take with her, with all the information right at hand. Back in her office, she could put the binder back on the shelf, making it easy to access. She had never thought about applying the system to other categories where binders make sense.

Next, we looked at the file cabinets and drawers. There was a reason why so much had piled up and she wasn't filing. Her filing drawers were completely overstuffed. Also, her personal files were mixed in with business papers. She had two long drawers, two small drawers, plus her desk drawer, so there were five drawers in total of filing, and the categories were all intertwined.

We designated one cabinet as her personal filing space for her home and personal papers; the rest were reserved for business. To eliminate the crowding problem, we took old files out and archived them into her basement storage area. With added room, and designated categories for business and personal papers, she now had a system that worked for her.

For active projects, we put a vertical filing stacker on her desk, so in addition to the to-do pile, which she still needed to subsort, all active projects were immediately accessible.

While it may appear to be complex, her system with binders, shelves, cabinets, vertical stacker, and an action inbox has worked well and has endured (see Figure 3-8) because each method within the system fits Margaret's needs.

When we talked about what had failed the first time she worked with an organizer and why the current system worked, we discovered that the primary difference lay in the initial process for sorting. Whereas I advocated the Three To's of sorting, she had previously been instructed to sort into all the different categories that were set up in her filing system. As a consequence, she had probably filed papers that should have been thrown out. While it took us sixteen hours to sort everything into the three simple piles, I wonder how long it would have taken her to sort into all the subcategories. We will never know because the thought of that detailed level of filing was too daunting, and the filing cabinets overflowed at the very start.

Just teaching Margaret to execute the Three To's methodology—to toss, to do, to keep—changed how she approaches filing. Now it is very doable and not overwhelming for her. One of the biggest mistakes people make is trying to go from no system to putting all the piles of diverse

Figure 3-8. Small office after. *Author's photo.*

papers into really specific categories. It's too hard, so only a few people even start getting organized this way, and rarely does anyone finish. Because the papers continue to mount, there is never time to catch up.

While the three-step sorting system works for anyone and any system, everyone needs to find the right filing containers and the best labeling and filing systems that work for each situation. There is no one filing system that works for everyone or every situation.

Once you have achieved physical organization, you are ready to begin the next level of the Peak Productivity Pyramid System—electronic organization.

PRODUCTIVITY POINTERS

- Physical clutter is the most common reason people look for productivity solutions. It is often the symptom of other productivity issues.

- The simplest way to tackle the buildup of physical clutter and to manage incoming papers is by sorting into three piles: to toss, to do, to keep.

- There is no one filing solution that works for everyone, so it is important to find one that works best for you. Often that means thinking outside the filing cabinet.

CHAPTER 4

LEVEL 2: ELECTRONIC ORGANIZATION

"I might as well save it . . . just in case . . . I might need it someday." More and more people are making the decision to save. But I'm not talking about the decision you make standing over the wastebasket with a letter in hand, a pile of out-of-date magazines, or a stack of clipped newspaper articles. It's the kind of clutter you can't see, not right away, at least.

It's the volumes of content available and easily accessible to us—content pushed to us from the Internet, information we grab as we go through the day. It's the proliferation of downloadable online media from iTunes and other sources, such as movies and podcasts; the rapid increase of online transmissions such as e-mail, e-zines, RSS feeds, and tweets; informational posts and articles on forums like blogs, Facebook pages, and LinkedIn. The proliferation of devices—smartphones, iPods, tablets, netbooks, laptops, and desktops—multiplies the onslaught of files exponentially. When a huge number of files are coupled with the steep drop in cost and seemingly infinite availability of storage, from iCloud servers to terabyte hard drives, more often people are opting to save rather than delete their electronic files. People aren't deciding at all; saving is the default action.

Electronic clutter is a result of the lack of decision making and can be the source of a great deal of stress. The other compounding issue of electronic clutter is where to save your electronic information so that it is retrievable. Electronic organization is not just about making choices regarding the amount of information you keep; it's also about being able to find the one item you need when you need it.

Clutter, whether it's physical or electronic, is usually the result of failing to make a decision about whether to delete, handle, or file something. If you're not making decisions about whether or where to keep items as they come in, you're creating clutter. Electronic clutter is becoming as much of a problem as physical clutter. Even when it's not an apparent problem, you are not operating at your optimum productivity unless you have skills for managing your electronic mail and filing systems.

Having systems for electronic organization is the next step (level 2) in the Peak Productivity Pyramid System. Without mastering electronic organization, it is highly unlikely you will progress effectively to the time management level (level 3). You can't manage your time effectively until you achieve electronic organization.

SEVEN WARNING SIGNS

When do you know if you have an electronic clutter problem? There are signs that let you know when you need to reassess how you're handling electronic files:

1. Exceeding your e-mail storage space allotted by your company or online system, such as the 7GB limit on Google Gmail
2. Feeling anxious about deleting something
3. Forgetting whether you saved something

4. Spending a lot of time searching for files because you don't know where you filed them or what you named them

5. Seeing a lot of icons on your computer screen with no rhyme or reason

6. Keeping thousands of digital photos, even the out-of-date, irrelevant, or bad photos, without any labeling system (other than date)

7. Keeping outdated and unread e-mail messages in your inbox[1]

One of my long-standing clients, Claire, returned to work after a two-month maternity leave. She works at a technology company and is quite savvy about digital tools. She even teaches classes to the general public. She initially called me because she was feeling overwhelmed about several upcoming deadlines on some major projects. She wanted to make sure that she was well positioned to accomplish everything on time.

During our first meeting, I asked lots of questions to assess her strengths and weaknesses and to identify where on the Peak Productivity Pyramid we needed to start. She had a small shared space for an office, but it was organized, clear, and neat. As our meeting started, instead of taking notes with a notepad and pen, she opened OneNote on her laptop and recorded our conversation as she typed notes. She told me about how she organizes her day, appointments, and tasks. She admitted that she is not especially detail-oriented and relies on her business partner to keep track of their to-dos. "I'm the executer," she said. "I get things done."

Then we started talking about digital organizing and how she maintains her files. She admitted that she accumulates all her files on her desktop and when it gets too busy and cluttered, she moves everything into a folder and dates it. That's all. There is nothing else that says what is in the folder. And there is no rhyme or reason—all of her files are in the folder together. Personal photos are stored with business documents; important information is stored alongside temporary draft files.

She explained, "When I upload pictures from my camera, I put them on my desktop because I need them in front of me, otherwise I'll forget to make a photo book. Then I have all my photos and other documents there and things get really messy. Then I can't find what I need for work. That's when I move everything into a folder and I just date it. Then I start over."

I made an observation. "So, you are doing electronically what people do with paper," I said. "You are creating electronic piles of papers."

She was excited about this revelation and said, "Yes, you are right! It's just like when friends were coming over and I had piles of paper everywhere, so I put them in bags, stuffed them in a closet, and never dealt with them again."

I told Claire, "There is nothing wrong with what you are doing, except lacking the follow-through. That's getting you overwhelmed. You're stuffing your pictures in a folder and forgetting about them." So I suggested, "What about just committing to work on your photo books once a week, maybe on Friday evenings if you find it relaxing. You have the intention, but you don't have the commitment. Once you schedule time, you go from intention to commitment."

Being technology savvy doesn't automatically make you electronically organized. The same systems that apply to physical organization, like keeping similar items together, making decisions about what to keep, and having systems in place to handle different types of items, also apply to electronic organization.

Some people have an excellent system to handle their e-mail but not their files or photos. Others may not handle their e-mail but have a well-organized electronic filing system. It's not always an all-or-nothing, organized or unorganized, electronic system. Let's look at streamlining the individual areas so that you can create more efficient, functional electronic systems.

ELECTRONIC FILES

It is usually easiest to first organize your electronic files. That step will provide you a basic structure for filing incoming items, whether they are e-mails, attachments from e-mails, audio, video, documents, or picture files. When organizing your electronic files there are two primary decisions:

1. How to structure your folders
2. How to name your files

Just as in managing your physical files, you need to decide what system you will use for your electronic folders and subfolders. The choices are similar:

- Client folders, which your computer will list alphabetically, if you start with the clients' last names
- Project files, organized by project numbers (for businesses that track proposals) and/or by numbers assigned sequentially
- Folders by date, because many businesses track by date
- Financial and other business operations files (e.g., staff, taxes, and so on)

The primary consideration in creating your structure is to think about how you will retrieve information. If your physical filing system (e.g., file cabinets or simple desktop folders) works for you, then you can mirror it for your online folder structure with confidence. This will help keep you organized online as well. Organizing your electronic file folders using the same names or categories you find useful for your paper files will be helpful to you when you retrieve something electronically.

Like physical files, you can also have folders within categories that give you even greater detail to clearly organize your online systems. You can have broad categories, with subfolders detailing the precise date, project, or type of files within that category.

Unlike physical filing, each file within an electronic folder needs to have a name and, specifically, a file name that will make it easy for you to retrieve. Without creating long, cumbersome titles, you need to be sure that when you want to retrieve a file, you will know exactly what folder, subfolder, and file name you've assigned. In physical filing, when you look at the piece of paper, you have a visual picture of what's on the paper: A letter has a date, company name, salutation. Papers contain information that immediately directs your attention to determine whether it is the correct item you are looking for. There are many options for online files that will help guide you to retrieve them, including:

* Keyword, title, project, or other descriptive terms
* Author who created (name or initials)
* Editor or collaborator (name or initials)
* Date
* Version number

If you find that you are frequently using the search function to find your files, then you are not naming, or organizing, your folders or files optimally. It is worth spending time to develop a system for file naming that works for you. The faster you can retrieve important information, the more productive you will be.

A, B, C'S OF E-MAIL PROCESSING

In a research study cited by an IDC Report by Susan Feldman, entitled *Hidden Costs of Information Work: A Progress Report,* the activities of e-mail consume an average of thirteen hours per week, per employee.[2] E-mail is intimately intertwined with document workflow, sales, scheduling, and nearly every other aspect of business processes. If you assume the average knowledge worker earns $75,000 per year, a company spends about $21,000 of that salary for that one employee to create, read, and answer e-mail. That's 28 percent of every employee's salary.

In 2008, AOL studied e-mail behavior[3] and found that people are checking their e-mail on dates, in their places of worship, and everywhere else imaginable, including:

- In bed, in their pajamas (67 percent)
- In the bathroom (58 percent)
- While driving (50 percent)
- In a bar or club (39 percent)
- In business meetings (38 percent)

That was in 2008, even before the massive proliferation of smartphones. Can you image the results of that survey if conducted today? In fact, a 2010 poll conducted by Tony Schwartz of The Energy Project, with the *Huffington Post,* revealed that 60 percent of participants spent less than two waking hours a day completely disconnected from e-mail.[4]

A 2009 report by Basex for Intel Corporation, entitled "Information Overload," says that an excess of information, resulting in an inability to concentrate on tasks and stay focused, is a massive problem in the twenty-first century, costing the U.S. economy $900 billion per year.[5] Intel has been researching and developing programs to deal with information overload for well over a decade. Its research shows that information overload results in eight hours per week in lost productivity for every knowledge worker, which, for a company Intel's size, means a cost of $1 billion per year. Here are some additional startling statistics mentioned by Intel:

- The typical Intel employee was receiving 50 to 100 e-mail messages daily.
- Employees were, on average, spending twenty hours per week handling e-mail.

- Thirty percent of e-mails were unnecessary.
- Top executives reported receiving up to 300 messages a day.
- Intel, as a company, received 3 million e-mails a day, on average.

These statistics show how important it is to have a good e-mail management system. Without one, you will realize a drop in productivity, an increase in stress, and a requirement to work more hours.

E-mail, however, is something we are just expected to handle. No one ever takes us aside and says, "Here is the instruction manual for handling e-mail." We are just expected to do it. Where most of us make a mistake is in not understanding the value of creating a system to process e-mail. As we learned in the chapter on paper management, having some kind of system that makes it easier and faster to process information is very important. There are some simple steps you can take to streamline your approach to e-mail and, ultimately, make you more productive. One method involves thinking of your e-mail handling system as the e-mail alphabet:

A = Access
B = Batch
C = Check
D = Delete
E = Execute
F = File

Access

The first step is to set up a schedule for accessing your e-mail at allotted times each day. Choosing when to process e-mail depends on what works best for you. Typically, though, checking e-mail four times a day tends to be enough for most people.

1. *First Thing in the Morning.* Usually people feel good about start-ing off their day by checking their e-mail, to make sure there is nothing urgent.

2. *Before Lunch.* There is a natural break at lunch time, making it a less disruptive time to check your e-mail.

3. *Midafternoon.* Another natural time to take a break is midafter-noon, when you are ready for a stretch or preparing to go off to a meeting.

4. *End of Day.* Before heading out from work, cleaning up as much of your inbox as possible means you will only have fresh e-mails to check in the morning. Knowing there were no last-minute emergencies left unhandled also means a less stressful evening for you and your colleagues.

Scheduling those four times each day, and allotting around fifteen minutes per processing session, tends to be enough, and least disruptive, for most people.

Batch

It is important to realize that these four times are for processing your e-mail. That doesn't mean you will respond in the moment to every e-mail that requires a response, or that you need to send every e-mail you plan to write in those fifteen minutes. You do need to recognize that the inbox is simply your batch of e-mail, sitting there waiting to be processed. Like that physical pile of mail, the inbox on your desk, it is a temporary loca-tion for storing your incoming e-mail. Your electronic inbox should be the place you receive your e-mail, and it stays there only until you pro-cess it.

It is worth mentioning that there is another school of thought that suggests you should not check e-mail first thing in the morning. The reason: We all know that e-mail can be a time drain, and when you check e-mail first thing, you'll get pulled into working on everyone else's priorities, not your own. However, I find people get anxious when they don't check e-mail first thing; they don't like not knowing what requests are coming in. When you process your e-mail using the A, B, C's method, you will be able to check e-mail first thing in the morning to give yourself peace of mind, without letting e-mail overwhelm or distract you.

Check

The next step is checking each e-mail, which doesn't mean you need to read each one. Often you can make a decision about an e-mail from the subject line or from the first few lines of the message. Much of the e-mail we receive comes as newsletters. If you are an industry analyst, a newsletter might be the most important document you read each day. For most of us, however, we can decide quickly whether it's important or even relevant.

Not all e-mail is meant to be responded to. Examples are those e-mails where your name is in a cc list or the subject line implies that it is an FYI type of message.

One of my clients, Phil, has a habit of responding to every e-mail. I started noticing that every time I sent him an e-mail, sometimes just as an FYI, I received an acknowledgment. The last e-mail from me was a meeting confirmation, where I wrote, "Great, that works for me, too. Thank you so much. I'll see you then." Then he replied, "Okay, it works for me, too." He felt the need to always respond even when my e-mail did not call for a reply. Have you ever received an e-mail thanking you for sending your thank-you e-mail? I often receive e-mail at two or three in the morning, then again at 6:00 a.m. The constant and immediate reply to e-mail is another clear symptom that e-mail controls someone's time and focus, and that the individual lacks an e-mail management system.

Letting go of the habit of responding immediately to the incoming e-mail ding, and instead learning to access your messages only four times a day, can be a challenge for some people. Becoming deliberate about processing and responding to e-mail, instead of reacting, is nonetheless an important shift that will lead you to a more productive day. Adopting this one electronic management strategy is worth your attention.

Checking your e-mail on a schedule will save you hours each week.

Delete

If your primary goal is to empty your inbox, one of the easiest ways to do that is to delete messages. You will process e-mail more quickly if you make the decision to delete as you check. If you read a newsletter and find that it is no longer relevant or has little to no value, then unsubscribe. You won't miss reading it, and you will no longer have to handle it. Delete everything that has no further action required. If you find that you are deleting everything that comes from a particular e-mail address, you should explore why. You might stop the e-mail from coming by asking the individual or organization to only send you e-mail that requires an action or response from you. Everyone should understand a request to stem the flow of unnecessary and unwanted e-mail messages.

Execute

Just as in organizing your physical papers, you only want to touch each e-mail once, if possible. If you only need a few minutes for replying or forwarding a message, then do it immediately. Messages confirming or scheduling an appointment, updating contact information, or answering a question or request should be handled immediately, if you can do so quickly.

The minute you realize that you will need additional information, or to involve others, or time to think, then you know that this is not a message you can handle immediately. You will have to take action at a later time. You might have to decide whether you are the one who should respond and take action. If you are not, then you can forward the message immediately to the right person. It might take time to figure out who the right respondent is before you assign or delegate the work. In this case, you will need to take action at a later time. Execute these e-mail messages that require further action by deleting or filing them and capturing only the relevant pieces of information in another location. You want to remove these e-mails from your inbox and capture the needed information somewhere else, in a system for tracking your projects, action items, and tasks, to make sure it gets accomplished. That is execution—making sure everything you need to do gets done.

File

If you cannot delete or execute (and move or delete) an e-mail, the next option is to file it. The primary reason to file an e-mail is if it is a record of something, a decision, an instruction, a status report, or something else you might need to refer back to at some future date. Failure to have the document to refer to would have adverse consequences.

There is no one right way to set up your e-mail filing system. You should set up a system that works for you personally. One way is to have subfolders within your inbox folder system. Your subfolders can be by topic, category, client, or project, depending on what kind of e-mail you receive. A lot of people like to have one folder called "Processed Items" so that every e-mail checked, deleted, or executed goes into that one folder.

Others like to extract e-mail from their mail system altogether by saving it as a PDF and filing it to their hard drive. Some people question whether they need to have folders at all in e-mail. After all, the search function for computers is getting more and more sophisticated. Still, it takes longer to search than if you know where your file is. It also becomes more difficult to delete obsolete files (a project that is completed, for example) when they are all interspersed.

The other advantage of having subfolders is the ability to set up filters that automatically move e-mail messages from the inbox into a specified folder. For example, if you receive a weekly status as an FYI from an organization that you only need to refer to sometimes, then you can automatically route the incoming e-mail to a project status subfolder. You never have to touch the e-mail, but you know exactly where it is when you need it. You can move all those enticing, distracting newsletters directly into a folder labeled "newsletters" to look at only when you have the time. If you have reports from staff that you need to roll up on a weekly basis, you can funnel them into a single folder, where they'll sit until you are ready to deal with them.

For e-mails where it is impossible, difficult, or politically unwise to unsubscribe, you can filter them into your junk folder or delete them automatically. Using filters can significantly cut the number of messages you handle at each session. It is well worth the time to learn how your e-mail system allows you to use filters.

Whatever system you choose for filing your e-mail, remember that the one place you should not be saving files to is your inbox. Remember, too, that e-mail doesn't have to be a 24/7 commitment. Keeping your inbox clear at regular but specific intervals should give you hours of additional time each week, decrease your stress from worrying about forgetting something, and increase your overall effectiveness at handling what is most important in a timely manner. It's as simple as remembering your A, B, C's.

BACKING UP YOUR FILES

As much as this chapter is about achieving electronic organization, the opposite extreme is failing to protect the files you have saved, especially files that are irreplaceable. Everyone knows someone whose computer has crashed or whose laptop was stolen; you've heard the sad story of how everything was lost: baby pictures, the wedding video, important project files, even sensitive data such as Social Security or credit card numbers.

Everyone should have a file backup system in place. For some records that companies scan into their systems, such as signed contracts or notarized documents, having a separate hard copy stored off-site is important. Most companies provide a central backup system for their employees' files and e-mail. For small businesses, there are a number of options. Online backup services offered by Mozy, Carbonite, and many other companies are even free for smaller amounts of storage space. You can look at comparisons of online backup systems on technical review sites like CNET to find one that fits your needs.

Even having a separate backup hard drive gives you two points of failure. It would be a rare coincidence that your backup drive and your computer would fail at the same time.

Online backup systems are favored, though, because they offer the added advantage of giving you the ability to access all your information anywhere, anytime. In the event of a fire, flood, or other disaster, the business could still access all of its files and continue to do business, despite being displaced physically. Like so many of life's contingency plans, these lessons are often learned the hard way. It's worth being proactive and figuring out how you can best protect your electronic files.

THE FUTURE OF ELECTRONIC MANAGEMENT

With the advent of cloud computing, sophisticated search capabilities, and increased Internet access speeds, we are already starting to manage electronic organization differently. With cloud computing, you do not need storage on your computer. In fact, you do not need a computer per se, just a device to access the Internet. Everything you need, including your applications, will be available through your connection to the Internet.

Spotify, Pandora, and iTunes are online music libraries with tens of thousands of songs available, but you don't see how they're organized. Behind the scenes, these sites create a directory structure with the artists' names, song titles, and album names. When you want to listen to a specific song, you can either search by artist or by the name of the song. These libraries will store playlists you create of your favorite songs that you can access whenever you want. Most of the sites will even suggest songs you might enjoy because of your listening habits, or automatically create playlists with the songs that you listen to the most or songs you've listened to most recently. You can search by style (genre) and you can tell your digital music service to play songs similar to what you are listening to. The system behind the scenes for these music sites is very intelligent and removes some of the work from the user. The system automatically gives you what you want, which would otherwise take a lot of time to compile or figure out on your own.

Online information systems are going to be even more intelligent in the future and remove more of the organizing burden from the user. You can already see it in the prompts from a Google search, where software algorithms handle much of the organizing and thinking about how to serve the information to the user. The systems behind iPhoto immediately recognize faces and locations so that you can search for all the pictures you took on vacation in California, or all the pictures that contain a certain person.

It will make life easier to have your desktop look just like a Google home page with a search box and then you enter a few words and your system retrieves the exact file you were looking for. While there are sophisticated tools that will enable us to organize lots of complex data, we will still need to adopt a mindset that fosters organization in order to use these tools. In the meantime, it is still important to have a structure and to have your information available at your fingertips, knowing where things are and how to find what you need, when you need it.

With a filing system for your papers and other physical items and an electronic system to organize your online life, you have the tools you need to tackle time management.

PRODUCTIVITY POINTERS

- Set up efficient electronic management systems. Don't let the availability of cheap digital storage take away the incentive to delete unneeded files.

- Check e-mail only at a few specified times each day. A schedule will free you up to execute what is most important to you, rather than what your e-mail tells you to do.

- Create organized, effective electronic systems that support your online needs and pave the way for streamlining your time management capabilities.

CHAPTER 5

LEVEL 3:
TIME MANAGEMENT

Congratulations! If you are reading this chapter, you are feeling confident in your achievement of physical organization and electronic organization. Now you are ready to begin living, which means making the most out of our most precious resource—time. Whether you're a janitor or the CEO of a multinational corporation, the reality is that you only have twenty-four hours in a day, and the number of days we have is limited. The next three chapters in this book are going to help you make the most of your time by aligning that time with activities that matter to you and are important for achieving your goals and reaching the level of possibility.

In the last twenty years, the amount of time Americans spend working has increased by 15 percent, with the average executive now working at least fifty-one hours per week. Meanwhile, our leisure time has decreased by 33 percent. That's according to a 2006 survey by NFI Research. We are trying to allocate the twenty-four hours we have each day to our daily activities of life while balancing all our responsibilities. Yet doing more of what you enjoy would improve your quality of life and help to manage your stress. Nearly everyone is feeling more and more stressed. Our tendency is to get everything done by working longer hours, but since time is finite, we are reducing time in other essential areas of our lives, such as family and friends.

Time management includes setting goals in key areas of your life by allocating time to those areas, working smarter not harder, and achieving the same results at work that you are achieving now while still being able to make time to do other important things. So, how do we get there? How do we achieve proficiency at the time management level?

THREE P'S OF TIME MANAGEMENT

In the next few chapters you will read about the three P's of time management:

1. *Plan.* Identify what you should work on, everything in your realms of need to do and want to do.
2. *Prioritize.* Identify what you should do first, second, or never.
3. *Perform.* It is one thing to know what you should do and another to do it. Performing means committing to your plan.

These three P's will move you toward a time management system that works for you. No one time management or organizing system alone is good for even one person. Even if you find a system that resonates with you, you might need to mix and match techniques, and get pieces of different systems, until you find what works best for any given moment. These chapters will give you the fundamentals as well as some of the simplest approaches to time management. Before starting, let's be sure we understand what time management is and isn't.

DEFINING TIME MANAGEMENT

In their bestselling book *Rework,* Jason Fried and David Heinemeier Hansson, the cofounders of 37 Signals, complain about workaholics, explaining that there are people who "try to fix problems by throwing sheer hours at them. . . . Working more doesn't mean you care more or get more done." They say that the real heroes are at home, even though the workaholics would like them to feel guilty for "merely working reasonable hours."[1]

You probably already have a definition in mind of what time management means to you, but it comes with many different meanings. Let's describe level 3, time management, in the context of the Peak Productivity Pyramid System.

Importance

Stephen Covey, in *The 7 Habits of Highly Effective People,* says, "What does it matter how much we do if what we're doing isn't what matters most?" Time management is about doing what matters most, first. It doesn't mean doing more things in less time. A lot of people come to my time management seminars hoping to learn tricks for accomplishing more in less time. In fact, time management is creating systems or systematic practices for doing what is of greater importance, even if that means doing fewer things. When you apply the Pareto principle, also known as the 80/20 rule, to time management, you will find that 80 percent of your accomplishments come from 20 percent of the activities that you do in a given day, week, month, or year. That's right, 20 percent of the tasks you do bring you 80 percent of your results.

Harold Taylor, in his book *Making Time Work for You,* defines time management as "the accomplishment of significant goals at the expense of relatively unimportant activities."[2]

We spend so much time working on the 80 percent—those urgent, seemingly important tasks, or the fires that we're putting out that aren't helping us achieve our goals. Good time management is about identifying the 20 percent of our tasks that will help us achieve what is most important and working on those first.

Choice Management

Another way to talk about time management is as choice management. We can't manage time. Time happens. We all have the same amount of time. We can, however, manage our choices in relation to the time that we have, what we choose to do with our time. In modern society, the increasing number of choices is having a big impact on our time. If you think about it, we have thousands of choices of things to do, own, dream about, and we want them all. We all have more things on our to-do list than we have time to do them all. Understanding what you shouldn't be doing and what you can say "no" to is just as important as knowing what you should be doing. Decision making has become a huge time consumer for us.

In his book, *The Age of Speed: Learning to Thrive in a More-Faster-Now World*, Vince Poscente cites how a "2006 poll revealed that only 26 percent of people claiming to be time-starved would choose having fewer things to do over having more time to do all the things they currently do."[3] We don't want to give up anything; we want to do it all. But there is a limited amount of time, so this is where time management comes in.

In our society, we are very focused on money. It's common for people to talk about having a financial budget. Most people have at least some sense of a monthly budget that they live by, but you never really hear people talking about having a time budget. Time is the only commodity that really matters. We don't elevate time to the same status that we elevate money, but you have to manage time like you manage money, or even better. You can always make more money, but you can never make more time. Individuals are starting to recognize time more and more as their most valuable, nonrenewable resource.

Just as with organizing, time management is a skill. It requires practice and it, too, takes time, like learning a new sport or how to play an instrument. The good news is that we are capable of excelling at time management. You just have to think long-term. You have to be committed to fixing systems and tweaking behaviors and routines, and just like with any other skill, the more you practice, the more you are aware of it, the better you'll become at managing your time.

PRODUCTIVITY POINTERS

There are many ways to define time management. Here are two useful ways to think about our relationship with time:

- Time management is doing what is important, those things that will lead you to fulfill your goals.
- Time management is about choice management, because we cannot manage time, we can only manage what we choose to do with our time.

CHAPTER 6

PLAN

Being busy does not always mean real work. The object of all work is production or accomplishment, and to either of these ends there must be forethought, system, planning, intelligence, and honest purpose, as well as perspiration. Seeming to do is not doing.

—Thomas A. Edison

You've probably heard the cliché that *failing to plan is planning to fail.* You can always change your plan, but you have to start somewhere. Having a plan allows you to better manage the choices you have. Do you know that the average office worker only spends 35 percent of an eight-hour workday on productive work? The rest of the time, or about five hours a day, is spent on any number of self-sabotaging things we do that keep us from being productive, such as looking for something needed, handling interruptions, searching the Internet, and reading e-mail.

The first of the three P's of time management stands for *planning*. That's the first step in becoming better at managing your time. You need to identify what you have to do in a day, a month, a year, or more. Think about it. You wouldn't start a big project at work without some planning. You wouldn't start a business without a well-thought-out business plan. Why, then, would you go through life without thinking about and organizing your activities and tasks?

Your calendar is the primary time management tool to use for planning. As Harold Taylor states in *Making Time Work for You,* "When you schedule your activities and tasks, you go from intending to do them to committing to execute."[1] Only once you've added a task or activity to your calendar, and carved out enough time to complete it, have you committed to doing it. Where do you start on your path to commitment?

WRITE DOWN EVERYTHING

Any time management book will tell you that the first step in planning is to get everything out of your head. You start by taking everything that is swirling in your mind and putting it all on paper or in your electronic system. Do a brain dump. Write down everything you can think of that is weighing you down and causing you stress. That includes anything you have to do: projects, tasks, little things, big things, personal things, birthdays, anniversaries, medical appointments, work things, family things, educational activities, financial things, volunteer commitments. Writing things down helps you to see the big picture and not feel stressed about forgetting something or expecting your brain to remember everything. Your brain should be freed to think strategically and execute your plan, not to try to remember everything you need to do.

Once you have cleared your mind of the swirling to-dos, it is time to look at your list and decide what you are going to do, when, and how. Start by quickly estimating how long you think it will take you to perform each task, project, or activity on your list. Be aware that we all tend to underestimate how long things really take. How often have you said, "I'll be there in two seconds," when in fact it took much longer? As a general rule, add about 30 percent to 50 percent more time than you think you will need. When you try to estimate or add up how long it will take to accomplish everything on your list, you'll quickly realize that you have a lot more on your plate than time to do it all.

FOUR DECISION CATEGORIES

Remember, time management is choice management. We all have much more to do than time to do it, so you need to look at all your activities and decide which ones to allocate time to.

There are four key ways to decide whether you will do something:

1. *Choose.* Identify what is important and essential for you to do.
2. *Remove.* You can take things off your list by saying, "No." You can decide not to do some things.
3. *Wait.* You can push back doing tasks or activities until next month or a few months from now.
4. *Delegate.* You can also delegate and have somebody else do something for you.

You choose to do a task or activity when you enter it on your calendar with time allocated to accomplishing it. Once you have made your plan, and you have added it up and decided what you are going to do, then you do it. As the saying goes, "Plan your work, then work your plan."

In nearly every time management system available, you will find that the first step is getting things out of your head and onto paper. Write everything down and do it often. You want everything out of your head because you don't want to burden yourself and your brain with having to constantly remind yourself of things you're supposed to do. You want your mind clear to think about bigger things: thinking strategically, being creative, coming up with projects, ideas, and different solutions. In his book *Getting Things Done,* David Allen calls it "mind like water."[2]

BETH'S STORY

When I was doing hands-on organizing, Beth called me to ask for help organizing her home office. She is a lawyer who, at that time, was working part-time for a law firm. Her husband was a full-time project manager for a construction firm. Through a confluence of events, she found herself overwhelmed by a problem that she had spent more than a year trying to solve. She is a mother of four children, ranging in age from infant to ten years old, which is why she was working just three days a week. In addition, at the beginning of the year the family had to do some major repairs and upgrades to the old home they had purchased a few years before. A new roof, new insulation, new insulated windows, and rewiring and remodeling the kitchen were the biggest projects. In the middle of the construction she became pregnant with her fourth child. It's a lot for anyone to fathom taking on.

There was one aspect of her daily routine that she always left to the end of the day, then the end of the week, and by the time she called me, it was a task she had put off till the end of the year: handling the mail. If something came in the mail that wasn't from someone she knew or recognized immediately with a handwritten address, then it went into a pile. The piles grew and grew, and the thought of even starting to sort through them was unbearable for her—and bear in mind that she is an intelligent, capable, successful person.

When we started, there was a year's worth of mail accumulated. She had already switched all the utilities to auto-pay systems because they had all been shut off at one time for delinquent payment. As we sorted through the mail, we discovered approximately forty credit cards, because she never canceled the automatic cards that came in the mail.

When we finally sorted through all of that year's worth of mail, we moved on to address another problem: There were strong indications that in addition to Beth's physical organization deficits, the root problem was in the area of time management. At work, she had an assistant who did everything for her: from scheduling appointments to reminding her of her daily schedule and handing her the papers she needed. When I started to assess what was going on, I discovered that she didn't have a calendar for her family life. When I asked how she kept track of doctors' appointments, she said, "They call the day before to remind me."

Some people are so smart that they are used to keeping things in their heads. However, when their world expands, it's nearly impossible to remember everything. In Beth's case, she was shuffling four kids to different events, activities, and doctors' appointments, on top of her work schedule and household management responsibilities. We found a paper planner to help her keep track of the family schedule and take to work for her assistant to coordinate with her work schedule. She had to learn to keep a schedule for herself, because she had never needed one before. Now she uses a smartphone along with an online calendar and reminders.

Beth is no longer overwhelmed. Sorting the mail is an ongoing task, something she completes daily. She no longer misses appointments, no longer has that stressful feeling that she's always one step behind and late.

As we discussed in the context of physical organization and electronic organization, delayed decisions lead to clutter. Mental clutter or even clutter in your calendar also delays decisions. Decide on actions and outcomes when things start to emerge on your radar instead of waiting till later. Try to make decisions right away so that you don't create mental clutter, physical clutter, or calendar clutter.

USING CALENDARS

One important key to planning for your greatest productivity is to choose a time management calendar and a task management system to use. There is no one system that is going to be right for everyone. Think about what works well for you. A lot of people are most comfortable with paper planners; others prefer to go all electronic. Most of my clients are relieved when they find out that I use a paper-based system. The medium doesn't matter. The most important thing when choosing your time management system is to pick one, and one only, and stick with it—unless you have a specific purpose for another time management system *and* are diligent about incorporating the schedules into your main system as needed.

Duplication is okay, as long as you have a reason to duplicate and you're able to do so completely. Most people make the mistake of having two or three calendars—for example, a personal calendar and a work calendar. You don't have two lives, and most of us can't be at two places at the same time; therefore, the easiest way for you to keep track of everything and understand what your day truly looks like is to have everything scheduled in only one calendar. You, your significant other, your children, and your aging parents—they all need to coordinate calendars, too. My husband and I sit down every Sunday night and review our calendars for the upcoming week, to ensure that everything we need to do is covered. We confirm that he will be home if I need him, and that there is no overlap in expectations of where we expect each other to be. I also do the meal planning that night, so I know who will be home when and so that I can do the shopping on Monday. This coordinated effort allows us to attack the week with purpose.

Another aspect of scheduling is finding the best time of day for completing different tasks. It is important to schedule big tasks for when you are most productive. Many people are most productive around ten o'clock in the morning. If that's true for you as well, you want to block off that precious time of 10:00 a.m. until 11:00 a.m., or 9:00 a.m. until 10:00 a.m. You want to schedule your time of greatest productivity for your most important projects because that is when your mind is thinking most clearly. You want to protect that time and not waste it with meetings, phone calls, checking e-mail, and other tasks that can be done at other times of the day when you're not as productive.

ONE LIFE, ONE SYSTEM

Perhaps you will recognize Anne. She is a married mother of two elementary school-age children, who works part-time in event planning at a local college while also running her household. When she was showing me her time management system, she opened the electronic calendar on her computer where she kept her work appointments. She also added her husband's schedule to her calendar by syncing his work calendar with hers. Then she pointed to a kitchen calendar where she kept personal and other family activities.

After asking her how her system was working, she confessed, "I'm always stressed out about missing things on the kitchen calendar. When I'm not at home, I forget to refer back to the family schedule. I'm embarrassed by how often I miss an appointment or am late and forget things."

She was missing a lot of important activities because she was never in the kitchen checking the calendar. She had it in the kitchen because when she was growing up, her mom had one there. Anne assumed that's what you had to do. It was a quick fix to incorporate her kitchen family calendar into her online calendar. With everything in one place, she could be on time for all her appointments and scheduled activities.

There is no right or wrong, there is no "have to," just what is right for you. The kitchen calendar might work great for stay-at-home moms who manage their family appointments and schedules activities. A kitchen calendar is always there for writing it down. But if you work, either away from the home or in a home office and already use an electronic calendar that you like, then commit to that system and use it for everything. With today's technology advances, such as smartphones, tablets, cloud computing, and Google calendars, there are many ways to integrate your personal and professional calendars.

That said, you can choose to use two devices for your calendar, as long as you are deliberate about it and avoid redundancy. Personally, I like to write everything down in a paper-based planner system. I like that feeling of the pencil on paper. It helps me remember better because I tend to visualize the page and think about where I wrote things. That's why I use a paper-based calendar system.

However, I also use my calendar on my smartphone. I have specific reasons for using one over the other, and I don't repeat tasks in both. I use my smartphone calendar for important things that I need reminders of, activities that have a date and time commitment to someone else, when I know I will be away from my desk and need the extra prompt. That includes recurring school-related activities for the kids, library books that need to be returned, and client phone calls I've scheduled that I need to make or be available for. Whereas I might not be near my planner or computer, I always have my smartphone close at hand and it reminds me. If I have an evening event or appointment that I do not want to miss, I send my husband a calendar invitation. Although I don't have access to his calendar, he can schedule my event and that way we can be sure the home base is covered. He relies completely on his work calendar and refers frequently to his synced iPhone and iPad. In fact, he is so dependent on this calendar that we have the understanding that if the event isn't on the calendar, I can't expect him to be there. If he can't make it to a particular event, he simply declines the invitation. This prompts us to discuss how we can make things work, for example, by getting a babysitter or making adjustments in our schedules.

Everything else that's scheduled, such as time to work on projects, exercise at the gym, events I need to attend, all go on my paper-based planner.

This system works for me. I'm not recommending this system to anyone, only offering it as an example of how you can use two devices (e.g., smartphone and paper-based planner) while still being efficient because you fundamentally have one system.

PAPER PLANNER

Several years ago, I worked with the marketing director for a big company that required everyone use the electronic Outlook calendar. The marketing director had been using a paper-based planner for many years and was very attached to it, so she continued to use it alongside Outlook by copying things from her electronic calendar to the planner. It took her a long time at the end of the day to copy everything and, of course, there was always the potential for mistakes. The two systems were redundant. There was no need for the paper-based planner in her life at work. Exploring why she felt the need for the planner revealed that, like me, she enjoyed writing things down. She acknowledged the extra time her redundant paper-based system required. Instead, we substituted a running notebook, where she would write down her tasks and to-dos so that she wouldn't forget. Additionally, she schedules time in her electronic calendar at work to block off tiers of time in which she needs to work on projects and tasks. This is another example to show that there are ways to integrate two methods, as long as you are deliberate and consistent about the role of each tool. You need to think about how to eliminate redundancy, and think about ways to keep track of things. When you find a system that accommodates your preferences, one that you feel comfortable using, then you will commit to the system and it will work for you.

TRACKING TASKS YOUR WAY

Again, there are several different ways to keep track of your tasks. A very simple, easy way is to keep a running list on a piece of paper or in a notebook by writing things down as they occur. Of course, you then schedule time in your calendar or planner, or your system for managing time, whatever you are using to schedule work on those tasks.

You can also use an electronic task system that integrates with your calendar by automatically scheduling tasks in your calendar. For example, if you use Outlook as an e-mail and calendar system, you can also use the Tasks function to keep track of tasks on your calendar. There are many different applications that help you create task lists on your smartphone or computer. Remember the Milk (rememberthemilk.com), toodledo.com, and todoist.com are several different websites that help you keep track of tasks.

Also, if you use a paper-based planner system, there are some planners that help you funnel tasks into your schedule—for example, The Planner Pad® and the FranklinCovey Planners.

No matter which system you choose, the most important thing is to stick with it, commit to using it, and remember to schedule time on your calendar to work on your tasks. Having a system for recording all your to-do items, and regularly making decisions for handling each one, paves the way for establishing priorities.

PRODUCTIVITY POINTERS

- Plan your calendar. Planning is choosing to do a task or activity by entering it on your calendar with time allocated to accomplish it.
- Write everything down so that you know everything you have to do.

- Decide how to handle each item on your to-do list: *choose* what's important, *remove* the item from your list, *wait* and do it later, or *delegate* the task.
- Select the right planning tool for you, whether it's a day planner or an electronic or physical calendar.

CHAPTER 7

PRIORITIZE

The second P of time management is to prioritize. In his book *The 7 Habits of Highly Effective People,* Stephen Covey said that "the key is not to prioritize your schedule, but to schedule your priorities." By prioritizing your tasks and all your to-dos, you get a clear sense of which activities in your life are moving you forward, toward your goals and toward important things, so that important things don't suddenly become urgent.

PRIORITIZING WITH URGENT AND IMPORTANT

In all my practices and research, one of the most enlightening concepts I have discovered is what Covey and others call the urgent/important matrix. Until I found this simple approach to establishing priorities, I found it difficult and complex to guide people through prioritization exercises. This one practice will make it much easier for you to prioritize your tasks every day and into the future. It helps you answer the simple question: What is most important for me to work on first?

While there are many variations and interpretations of the urgent/important matrix, the most prominent time management expert in Brazil, Christian Barbosa of Triad Productivity Solutions, took the urgent/important concept one step further. He added the realm of circumstantial to it, creating what he calls the Time Management Triad. "Circumstantial" refers to unnecessary activities, social obligations, and time wasters. You might want to include that category as you use urgent and important to prioritize your list of activities.

Figure 7-1 is a modified way to look at the urgent/important matrix that I have honed as a result of my using and adapting it in training and coaching. It is central to the rest of the discussion that follows.

Let's start by understanding what we mean by important and urgent:

- *Important* activities are of greatest significance or value. They are likely to have a profound effect on your success and will lead you to achieving your goals.
- *Urgent* activities demand immediate action or attention, but they are often not associated with your goals.

Using these two terms will help you decide which activities to do first. We have defined productivity as *doing what matters most, first,* and spe-

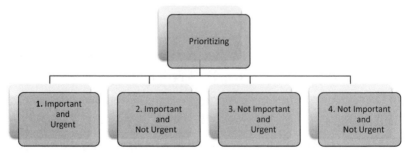

Figure 7-1. Prioritizing with urgent and important.

cifically, *doing what will move you most quickly to meet your goals.* When you are planning your activities and prioritizing what you are going to do, first focus on activities that are important—that is, those activities and tasks categorized in the Important and Urgent and Important and Not Urgent boxes, as shown in Figure 7-1.

Box 1: Important and Urgent

Activities that you list in box 1 are necessary for you to do. For example:

* *Crises and Other Deadline-Driven Emergencies.* No matter how carefully you plan, emergencies will come up unexpectedly. You have to spend time addressing those issues, even though they may not necessarily be planned or scheduled on your calendar. In fact, depending on the level of importance and urgency, you may find yourself bumping other items off of your calendar in order to get these items done.
* *Critical Meetings.* The ones that are essential to moving your career or projects forward.
* *Project Deadlines.* Not the kind that are self-imposed but instead are essential to meeting commitments or have adverse consequences when you miss them.

What you will find is that it is much easier to incorporate Important and Urgent tasks and make choices about managing them when you have a clear vision of what your day or your week looks like.

Box 2: Important and Not Urgent

This category is where success happens. In box 2 in Figure 7-1, you will list tasks such as:

- *Preparation and Strategic Planning.* Think about your personal goals, business goals, and your company's goals. Long-range planning should be undertaken in order to minimize or eliminate disruptive Important and Urgent activities.
- *Working on Projects.* Plan your work to avoid projects becoming deadline-driven and causing problems.
- *Training and Professional Development.* These are activities essential to your growth and achieving future goals.
- *Exercise, Relaxation, and Self-Care.* Make sure you schedule these Important and Not Urgent activities in your calendar so that they become priorities for you.

Box 3: Not Important and Urgent

You want to avoid most things classified as Not Important and Urgent. These are the activities that cause unnecessary stress. Box 3 in Figure 7-1 is where you will find the following kinds of activities:

- *Opportunities with a Deadline.* Sometimes there is an opportunity that requires your action within a specific time frame to take advantage of it. Because of the sense of urgency that a tight deadline causes us, it is easy to mistake the opportunity for something important. Make sure you step back and really question whether it is a true opportunity or simply another task that will waste your time.
- *Requests for Information or Help.* People will ask for help or for information with a sense of immediacy, and it's hard to say no.
- *Self-Imposed Deadlines.* Too often people set impossible deadlines needlessly for their own projects or deliverables.

Box 4: Not Important and Not Urgent

You want to avoid everything classified as Not Important and Not Urgent (box 4 in Figure 7-1), where you will find the following kinds of activities:

* *Interruptions.* People walking in unannounced, unscheduled phone calls, and distracting thoughts are common examples.
* *Telephone Calls.* Here I'm referring to calls, including social calls, that have no purpose, provide no information, or require no action.
* *Meetings.* Poorly run meetings without goals, actions, or information.
* *Trivial Busy Work That Occupies or Wastes Your Time.* These are the activities that we do when we are avoiding real work. They include paper shuffling, procrastination, surfing the Internet, using social media such as Twitter and Facebook, and even watching TV.

Too often we waste much of the time that we have. On average, Americans spend about thirty hours a week watching television. While I like a good TV show as much as the next person, and TV as entertainment certainly has its place in the downtime category, there are too many people who simply sit in front of the TV for countless hours, with no particular purpose. That is time that could be used moving you toward your goals; it is time better spent achieving higher-level thinking or completing projects and tasks that are weighing you down. You want to avoid things that are Not Important and Not Urgent in your life. You want to focus your energy on essential tasks, activities, and projects that are going to have the greatest impact on your success, your career, your happiness.

Think about the analogy of filling a glass jar. You have to put in the rocks, then the pebbles, then the sand, then the water, because if you fill the glass with water first, there's not going to be room for anything else. So, if you think of the rocks and pebbles as your important activities and projects, and you fit those into your calendar first, then the sand and the water will fit in wherever you have room for them.

Ultimately, you will get to a point in your life where you are going to be a lot more comfortable saying no, eliminating activities that are just time wasters for you, or minimizing unimportant tasks. The more you practice your time management skills—the more you practice scheduling your priorities, instead of prioritizing your activities—the better you will be at realizing when something is not important, and you just won't do it.

The more you learn about time management and understand the value of your time, the more you will protect it and not let others "steal" your time with interruptions, unnecessary chatter, and meaningless activities.

Prioritizing your activities according to what is urgent and important will help you be more aware of what you should be doing on a daily, weekly, monthly, and yearly basis, which will allow you to work on the tasks that will lead you to achieving your goals. It will also help you to clarify what goals you need to set on your journey when you maximize the time you have to accomplish what matters most to you. By paying more attention to how you spend your time, you become more aware of how to direct your efforts to more important work.

PRODUCTIVITY POINTERS

- Prioritize your tasks and activities. It will ensure that you do those things that matter most.
- Look at each task and activity in terms of its urgency and importance.
- Become more aware of how much time you spend on activities that distract you from what is most important.

CHAPTER 8

PERFORM

The third P of time management is *perform*. Once you have planned and prioritized, you have to perform. You have to *plan your work, then work your plan*. There are several things that keep us from performing at the optimal level. I call them time wasters. Examples include perfectionism, multitasking, procrastination, interruptions, looking for things, meetings (sometimes), and too much time spent in choice management. These are all things that derail us from working our plan. The only way to avoid these time wasters is to recognize and develop strategies for dealing with them.

PERFECTIONISM

Many of the people I have worked with are highly successful executives and entrepreneurs. Among highly successful people, there is often a tendency to pursue perfection, which frequently leads to successful but suboptimal outcomes. We focus on doing things right. Some of us even experience perfection paralysis, which means that if we are not completely sure how to do something or don't believe we are capable of doing it to perfection, we won't do it at all.

We need to focus on doing the right things adequately instead of doing everything right. We should focus our perfectionism efforts on things that really matter or on our biggest priorities. In parenting, or when performing for an event, for example, of course you strive for perfection, because these things are especially important to you. But in most tasks and projects, we need to focus on doing the right things adequately. Michael J. Fox made the distinction so eloquently when he said, "I'm careful not to confuse excellence with perfection. Excellence I can reach for; perfection is God's business."

Think about doing the right things adequately as striving for excellence, not perfection. Or think about adopting this slogan: DONE IS BETTER THAN PERFECT.

OVERCOMING PROCRASTINATION

Procrastination means, according to its Latin root word, "putting forth tomorrow." Procrastinating is delaying to start or finish a task (or several tasks) that should be a priority. The ability to overcome procrastination and tackle important actions can have the biggest positive impact on your life, and it is one of the chief hallmarks of the most successful people. So how do you overcome procrastination?

First, it is important to understand why you procrastinate, and there are several different possible reasons. Here is a list of some of the most common:

- Lacking clarity regarding deadlines, resources, or where to begin
- Seeking the thrill of the last-minute rush
- Feeling overwhelmed by the task

- Lacking the initiative to get started
- Fear of success or failure and how that reflects on you

In *Eat That Frog*, Brian Tracy says, "In the business world, you are paid and promoted for achieving specific, measurable results. You are paid for making valuable contributions that are expected of you. Confusing activity with accomplishment is the source of one of the biggest problems today, which is failure to execute." When we are busy doing a lot of mundane activities, often we are actually procrastinating. We are avoiding work on the big projects or important activities that we are getting paid for; we are avoiding what could be our biggest accomplishments. Tracy stresses working on what's most important. He writes, "Your ability to select your most important task at any given moment, and then to start on that task and get it done both quickly and well, will have more of an impact on your success than any other quality or skill you can develop."[1] If you nurture the habit of setting clear priorities and getting important tasks finished quickly (and excellently), the majority of your time management issues will simply fade away.

There are ten different ways to overcome procrastination. These strategies are not new, and you will likely find them in other places, but they are worth repeating.

1. *Delete.* Think about the 80/20 rule, where 20 percent of your activities are bringing you 80 percent of your results. Is what you're working on something that really needs to be done? What are the consequences of not doing it? Perhaps you should delete the activity so that you can move on to what is important.

2. *Be positive.* Procrastination is usually tied to negative self-talk, or when you say things such as "I have to," "I should," "I must finish." Changing this self-talk to messages of choice and commitment helps overcome procrastination. Instead, learn to say "I

will" or "I choose to." Switch your energy from your procrastination self-talk to the language of the producer.[2]

3. *Take the first step.* If you start the task right now, you remove all the anxiety and feelings of stress. As soon as important activities and tasks come up, make the decision to schedule time in your calendar to at least start the task, or to ask for advice, if needed. That way you will be able to get it done as early as possible.

4. *Ask for help.* When lack of clarity causes procrastination, sometimes asking for help is all you need to do. A trusted mentor, a supervisor, a coach, or somebody else you trust can provide clarification, insights on where to start, or outline steps for completing the project.

5. *Break it down.* Break down large projects into actionable steps. Huge assignments don't look as big broken down into the smallest steps possible. Make sure that you are entering actionable tasks into your calendar. Don't just write down "Presentation," because that is not a task. Creating a presentation can be broken down into clear and manageable tasks; for example: 1) do research, 2) create outline, 3) develop content, 4) put into PowerPoint, and 5) practice. For an entry like "Presentation," you probably need at least two hours in your calendar, which is not easy to find. The five smaller tasks are very actionable because you know exactly what you need to do. The smaller blocks of time required for each task will be much easier to schedule into your calendar.

6. *Follow the twenty-five-minute rule.* To reduce the temptation of procrastination, each actionable step on a project should take no more than twenty-five minutes to complete. This rule is based on the Pomodoro Technique, which is a time management tool created by Francesco Cirillo. The concept, as he developed it, is to use a timer and only work in twenty-five-minute increments, taking short breaks between each segment, then a longer break

after four segments of work. This technique is especially useful at those times when we are overwhelmed or have to do something we don't really want to do. Knowing that we're only going to work on that task for twenty-five minutes, and once the timer goes off, we can give ourselves a reward, makes working for those minutes easier and the task more manageable.

7. *Give yourself a reward.* Celebrate the completion of project milestones, and reward yourself for getting projects done on time. It can be a coffee break or a little time on Facebook or Twitter, or it can be a big reward. Whatever it is that you want or that makes sense, a reward provides positive reinforcement and motivates you toward completing your project.

8. *Set and respect deadlines.* If you haven't been given a deadline for a project, ask for one or assign yourself a deadline, and write it down in your calendar. Make your deadlines known to other people who will hold you accountable. Procrastination is much more likely with no real deadline. Creating your will is a classic example. Nobody plans on dying, yet we all know that we're going to, and there is no clear deadline for dying, so people tend to procrastinate activities associated with preparing for death. Yet, it is important to create a will, especially if you have children. If you impose a deadline (for example, I am going to complete my will by December 31), it helps you get things done. Completing tasks that you've been procrastinating, especially one as morbid as estate planning, will liberate your mind from that nagging feeling that you are not being responsible.

9. *Remove distractions.* You need to establish a positive working environment that is conducive to productivity. Remove any distractions. If you are having a hard time working on a task or project, having a lot of distractions is only going to help you make excuses to not work on it. Access to the Internet, nearby people available

for chitchat, the phone ringing, e-mail pop-ups—all of these things are going to cause you to procrastinate. Therefore, remove all distractions for at least twenty-five minutes and work.

10. *Be accountable.* Having an accountability partner is one of the best ways to stay on track with tasks and projects. In his book *Still Procrastinating?* Joseph R. Ferrari tells the story of a Harvard economics professor who paid his coauthors $500 when he did not deliver a promised paper or finished product by its due date. Having a financial consequence certainly helps curb procrastination, but you don't have to go that far. Most times, simply having someone follow up with you on a promised task is enough to keep you on track.

TIME WASTERS

When I moved to the United States as a college student, I was in charge of doing my own grocery shopping for the first time in my life. The first time I walked through a supermarket, I will never forget turning the corner and seeing the cereal aisle. There was a whole aisle dedicated to cereal. I love cereal. In Brazil, we had two options: Frosted Flakes or plain, unfrosted cornflakes. That was it, and that's what we bought. In Brazil, you typically don't eat cold cereal for breakfast, you eat a hot breakfast. But I love cereal, and I remember being in that aisle for hours reading every box and discovering the brands I'd never seen before. I wanted to try all of them.

Looking back, it was so easy in Brazil with only two choices: You either bought one or one of each, and that was it. Having so many cereal choices and deciding which brands to try, while wonderful for a cereal lover like me, was so much more daunting. Until I had three kids, the cereal aisle was a pleasurable, if not somewhat odd, distraction for me. But having all those choices was also a huge time drain.

Another term for distractions is *time wasters*; here are some other time wasters and some ideas for how to avoid them.

Multitasking

As life became more complicated, with more choices, more things to do, everyone started searching for ways to do things faster, instead of questioning the things that they were doing. Multitasking became popular in an attempt to keep up. The truth is that working on two or more jobs, tasks, or projects at the same time reduces the efficiency of each effort. David Meyer, a researcher, claims that not being able to concentrate on one task for significant periods of time may cost a company as much as 20 percent to 40 percent in efficiency.

Brain scan studies reveal that if we perform two tasks at the same time, we only have half of our usual brainpower devoted to each task. So when we multitask, we're only half there for each activity. The truth is, we can't do two jobs simultaneously. Our brains aren't capable of focusing on two separate things at the same time. Instead, the brain switches rapidly between one task and another, which causes us stress and to lose concentration, as it takes time for the brain to refocus and concentrate on one task and then the other. Multitasking becomes ineffective and ultimately counterproductive.

In 2006, there was a survey conducted by Basex showing that 50 percent of employees were writing e-mails or instant messages during conference calls. You've probably been guilty of talking on the phone and trying to read e-mail at the same time, and the more complex the tasks being worked on simultaneously, the greater the chance of error, and the greater amount of time consumed in the transition from one task to the other. There are things you can do at once, like watching TV while wrapping presents, or listening to music while working out. It might take a little bit longer with the TV or music on, but it doesn't matter because there are no real consequences. But if you are trying to review a contract while talking on the phone with someone, there are more likely to be errors that impact the bottom line of your business. In our effort to get more done in less time, rather than doing the right things in the amount of time that we have, we sabotage ourselves.

When you are trying to listen to your voice mail while reading your e-mail, or reading other materials during meetings, multitasking is working against you. Instead, you need to identify the priorities, the tasks, the important things you need to work on, and work on them one at a time. Again, time management isn't about doing more things; it's about doing more of the important things.

When you implement the e-mail management processing system we discussed in the chapter on electronic organization, where you're checking e-mail at set intervals of three or four times a day, you won't be checking it during phone calls or meetings. If you are tempted to multitask, either check whether a task can be eliminated altogether or carve out a specific time on your calendar to dedicate to doing the task. Otherwise, you will find yourself wasting your day away doing things in a less productive manner.

You might come across some more recent research that claims to show how multitasking can be effective. What the researchers are actually talking about is something more correctly called *duo-tasking,* a term that emerged a couple of years ago and is gaining more recognition in the time management world. Duo-tasking means you start a task and put a task into action while you do something else. You can delegate a task to someone who completes it while you work on something else.

Tom, a CFO of a technology start-up, is a high performer who always wants to improve. As with many of my other clients, the work we do together is not focused on fixing a deficit in productivity but rather improving a strength. Tom's responsibilities are far-reaching and impact many areas of his company. One example of duo-tasking that comes to mind was his experience getting ready for a critical board meeting. He created the framework for the financial model that he needed to present and had his controller fill in the appropriate numbers while he focused on getting the deal documents ready for board review.

When you duo-task, your focus is not on switching back and forth; you just set one task in motion as you're working on another task. There's no lack of focus, so there is no risk involved. You're setting a task in motion while you concentrate and work on something else. It is not true multitasking, where you are going back and forth between activities, trying to work on two things simultaneously.

Interruptions

There are two primary ways we experience interruptions. The first is externally; we are interrupted by somebody or something else. For example, someone walks into our office, calls, or sends an e-mail. The second way we experience interruptions is internally, when we interrupt ourselves. Examples include checking your e-mail before schedule, getting up to refill the coffee cup, and browsing the Internet. Self-interruptions occur especially when we are procrastinating. Whether you welcome them or not, such interruptions will disrupt your productivity. Become more aware of interruptions and you will begin to see just how much they affect your work.

There are a few ways you can cut down or eliminate external interruptions or minimize the time spent with other people who are interrupting you:

- *Close the door.* If you have an office, close the door when you need focused, productive work time.
- *Create clear signals.* If your workspace doesn't have a door (especially as more and more workspaces are designed to be completely open to foster communication and team building), then create

clear signals of when you are open to being interrupted and when you're not. Use whatever method works for you. For example, you could wear headphones as a signal that tells other people, "When I have headphones on, I don't want to be interrupted." Some companies invest in high-end headphones for employees to use in these open environments. You can either have a companywide rule or create your own rule that everybody is aware of.

- *Post a sign.* Hang up a sign somewhere on your cubicle that says, "Please don't interrupt me now."
- *Walk a person out.* If somebody comes into your office and tries to talk to you, you can very quickly and nicely end the conversation by saying, "Oh, I'm so sorry. I'm working on a project now. I'll stop by your desk later and we can chat," or "How about we do lunch together?" If someone walks in and sits down to talk to you, often standing up and moving toward the door gives the other person a signal to leave. Walk the person out with you as you go to the restroom. You can walk people out by literally escorting them or by using words to let them know that now is not a good time for interruptions.

If you are self-interrupting and find yourself stopping your work too often and at unscheduled times to check e-mail, Facebook, your fitness app, or to make phone calls, that is a problem that's harder to overcome. Handle phone calls just as you do e-mail. Set times during the day when you return or make important calls. If you are checking e-mail four times a day, then you could tie in checking voice mail during the same scheduled time frame. Return calls immediately that require a quick conversation of two minutes or less. If it's going to become more of a project or conversation, schedule the call in your calendar. When you schedule your phone calls outside of your highly productive times, you build logic around your day and avoid unnecessary interruptions. You're making choices, purposeful decisions about how you're going to break out your day and schedule your time.

Do not let others hijack your most valuable, nonrenewable resource. If other people are interrupting you, or if you are self-interrupting, you are giving away or letting others steal time from you. You can avoid that by creating routines, which is one of the best ways to streamline your time management, making it second nature and part of your day. Schedule phone calls for right after lunch every day, or whatever time is convenient for you. If you have an assistant who schedules your calls, communicate your preferences clearly.

Alex runs a public relations and marketing company and has several employees. His business requires him to have monthly check-in phone calls with all his clients. He wakes up very early, around 4:00 a.m., and starts his workday then. By three in the afternoon, he stops working, because he finds it too difficult to focus and do productive work after being fully engaged in business activities for almost twelve hours.

His assistant, however, was scheduling two or three client calls a day. The last call was being scheduled for 2:30 or 3:00 p.m., when he was supposed to be finished working. After each call, Alex had to make notes and transcribe information from the call. At that point he was too tired mentally to transcribe them, so it would spill over into the next day when he couldn't quite remember all his notes. Switching the last scheduled call of the day to 2:00 p.m. at the latest made a huge difference. He is much less stressed now, and work no longer spills into the next day. If there is an international client or an exception that needs to be made, he can purposely make a choice to break the plan and start working later. It is an important shift from something just happening and you reacting to it to making a specific choice and taking control of your day and using the power that you have to control what you do with your time.

STEALING TIME

More and more nowadays, you see people stealing time. For example, parents are stealing family time or employees are stealing company time. How often do you go out to dinner and there is a family seated at another table a short way from you? They are waiting to have their order taken, and you see the husband, or the wife, or both of them stand up and take a work call. Maybe you're at a soccer field watching your kid's game and you're checking your e-mail. When you do that, you are stealing time from something that's important: your family. You are trying to fit everything in, but you are interrupting your time with family by doing something else.

Your day is not clearly defined. Of course, crises happen, and there are days when you are going to have to be on the phone or checking e-mail, but most of the time these are not important or critical things that you have to do at that moment. This has become the natural way we conduct business these days, because there is no clear definition between work and personal life anymore. Many of my executives resist this criticism and initially tell me that I don't understand the demands of their jobs. I usually challenge them to discipline themselves for one week. When we meet again, they report tremendous increases in productivity and satisfaction.

Everything spills over because we are so connected. We take our laptops and our smartphones everywhere with us. When you are prioritizing and scheduling your tasks and activities, be sure to have a clear definition of when and where you will be fully present so that you avoid stealing time away from what is most important. That is one of the most important time management lessons: Be fully present in that choice that you made with your time at that moment.

Having greater awareness of how you are spending your time, and of your greatest inefficiencies, is one step toward a more productive you.

The most important thing you can do to ensure you are allocating the most time to those activities and tasks that are most important is to align what you do with the goals you set for what you want to accomplish.

PRODUCTIVITY POINTERS

- Be aware of the biggest time wasters to avoid the traps that distract you from your goals. Even the easiest and most accessible time management system won't help if you don't perform.
- Commit to do what you plan to do.
- Find the best ways to overcome procrastination; understand which rewards or accountability actions work best for you and help you perform.
- Avoid multitasking, which makes you less efficient.
- Plan how you will deal with your most frequent interruptions.
- Beware of stealing time and its downside.

CHAPTER 9

LEVEL 4: ACTIVITY-GOAL ALIGNMENT

Alice came to a fork in the road. "Which road do I take?" she
  asked.
"Where do you want to go?" responded the Cheshire Cat.
"I don't know," Alice answered.
"Then," said the Cat, "it doesn't matter."

— LEWIS CARROLL, *Alice in Wonderland*

Katy is married with two kids, and she runs her own business, a franchise gym called Anytime Fitness. The gym is open 24/7, which is the key differentiator that makes her gym more appealing to businesspeople in the area. While the gym is not staffed 24/7, members have a key so that they can work out anytime, and the facility is armed with security cameras and other safety measures.

Katy was an owner of the Anytime Fitness club for five years when she first approached me for help. She called me on a Sunday while feeling even more frazzled than usual. She was trying to organize all her tax information for the accountant while also tending to her usual duties at the gym. She hadn't done anything to prepare all year, and here she was, on a Sunday, taking time away from her family because she had to get all these things done. She knew she needed to be more in control and more productive.

From our first meeting it was clear to see that Katy is someone driven to be the best she can be. She wasn't even looking at all the good things she was accomplishing; instead, her focus was on everything that wasn't getting done.

I asked her, "Is this where you thought you would be after five years in your business?"

And she said, "No, absolutely not. We thought that five years in, we would have a second location, that things would be great. Instead we're kind of struggling a little bit."

So I asked her, "How many members do you have now?"

She replied, "About seven hundred."

I said, "How many members do you need to keep things going well, so you're not worried about paying your rent and other fixed operating costs every month?"

She said, "Nine hundred."

And I said, "Have you ever had nine hundred members?"

"No, it's fluctuated between seven hundred, seven-fifty, and six hundred and eighty," she replied. So immediately, we set a goal. We didn't start at the bottom of the pyramid, because there was very little work to do on the physical and electronic clutter tiers, based on my assessment. The electronic skills were mostly tied to time management, which is where she needed the most help with her skills. While we worked on time management, we focused on the business goal of attaining 900 gym members by the end of our second year working together.

Having that focus changes the way Katy does things.

Ordinarily, her day is filled with interruptions. When she's in the office, her door is always open, with visitors coming in and out. She's a highly social person, and people are naturally drawn to her. She also needs to be there for her clients and staff. Unfortunately, this means when she's sitting down to work on a project, it's very difficult for her to focus.

Here we were, talking about the primary goal for her business—a goal that was critical to the viability of her business and her livelihood—and we realized how little time she was spending to achieve this goal.

Katy's issue was clearly one of poor activity-goal alignment.

Eighty percent of her day is consumed with interruptions, so we began working on minimizing them. We started by conducting weekly rounds of the facility to stock adequate supplies: the vending machines, the locker rooms, and the front desk. We blocked off time in her calendar to do specific repetitive, routine activities that would otherwise lead to interruptions. For example, when a member comes in and says, "We're out of water in the vending machine," she's interrupted and time is wasted. By preventing that sort of emergency, she is much more effective.

Our first step was to create a structure to her week, which falls into the time management tier of the Productivity Pyramid. Because Katy now blocks time during her week, she knows that Monday is the day for doing facilities and membership updates from the prior week. She also has blocks of project time built into her calendar. Having structure, knowing what she should be working on when, puts her more in control.

Adopting a deliberate structure to her week allows her to devote sufficient, and effective, time to achieving her most important business goal, expanding the membership base. Through the gym's website, Katy receives automatic reminders to make calls every day to potential gym members who expressed interest in receiving more information. When we first started working together, Katy was more than sixty calls behind. If her main goal is to increase membership, making follow-up calls is one of the things she has to do. We set a goal of ten calls a day and blocked off time in her calendar. Not only have the calls helped to bring in new members, but keeping the number of calls manageable on a daily basis has eased her mind and made her more effective on each call. Instead of thinking she has sixty calls to complete, a number that is too overwhelming to tackle, she only thinks about completing ten a day and makes the calls.

When looking for other ways to support her sales goals, we discovered that the franchisor provides a corporate consultant who advises franchisees on how to market the business. We planned time to reach out and use the consultant's suggestions to more effectively market to other local businesses. Katy came up with the idea of creating special enrollment plans for these companies. She delivered the information by way of a goodies basket that's delivered with the brochures inviting corporate memberships. Her goals include delivering five baskets each week to candidate companies. Delivering the baskets alone is not enough, so we allocated time on her schedule each week for follow-up calls.

Little by little, everything Katy is doing each week is aiming toward her goal of 900 members. She's doing little things every week with that big goal in mind. She's tweaking her system as she goes, as needed. Once she feels completely in control and comfortable in her progress toward her goals, then she will be ready to expand her goals.

LIFE-CHANGING SKILLS

When you hone your skills at the bottom of the Peak Productivity Pyramid, you become organized and you create the systems you need to help you to manage your environment better. Then you work to achieve time management and you operate more efficiently. All of those skills change how you manage your day, and you feel in control. But it's not until you develop goals, and align them with what you choose to accomplish every day, that you start making big changes in your life. You will find yourself living your life with purpose, making choices every day that change your life.

While the Peak Productivity Pyramid System sets forth a progressive framework, it is an iterative process toward what I call "possibility." After you achieve physical organization and move toward electronic organization, you might go back and find ways that you can further improve your physical organization skills by adopting new technologies—for example, by scanning documents into your electronic system to eliminate the paper files.

When you move from electronic organization to time management, you might need to tweak your electronic systems to accommodate changes in your time management strategies. It is likely that you will backslide and revisit each tier as you move up the pyramid. Not only is this backslide acceptable, but it is entirely appropriate and will further improve your skills in each area. Think of it as taking one step backward to take two forward. These skills are interdependent and do not exist in isolation. Once you become organized and set up systems, you are never quite finished because life is happening, your goals change, new technologies emerge, and your priorities change as well. You will always tweak and make improvements, always get even better. Each time you learn new skills, you will find ways to improve your efficiency throughout the Peak Productivity Pyramid System.

WHY GOALS ARE IMPORTANT

One of the main reasons I started my consulting business is because I want to help people live a life with purpose. Dictionary.com defines purpose as "an intended or desired result." Living a life with purpose means living each day thinking about the desired outcome. To do that you need to take a step back from the chaos of everyday life and see the bigger picture. What do you want to be when you grow up? I want to help people make sure that the choices they make every day are leading to something bigger—to their vision of who they want to become.

The indispensable first step to getting things you want out of life
is this: Decide what you want.

—BEN STEIN

What I have observed is that with all the noise and chaos surrounding them, many businesspeople find it extremely difficult to take that step back and focus on their vision, on their short-term and long-term goals. The demands on their time and schedule are such that it does not allow for focus on strategic planning and goal setting.

Their businesses are successful, and they are getting more and more clients and having to hire more employees. Their families are growing in size, and their children participate in so many activities. Their health and fitness strategies fall to the sidelines and their days are spent putting out the most urgent fires. They run around like a hamster in a wheel.

Even though they want to live a life with purpose and develop or update their goals, having this added task on their ever-growing to-do list is a source of stress rather than relief. Even if they do carve out time to develop their goals, it is usually in a rush to get it done and cross it off the list. After all, they have an accountability partner (me) coming back soon to check on their status. They never take the time to really consider all areas of their lives and decide what is most important for the short- and long-term. That is when I have to quote Will Rogers, who said, "A vision without a plan is just hallucination."

Setting goals doesn't have to be overwhelming. What if the day-to-day tasks that you do actually move you toward your goals? Sometimes, becoming aware of how setting goals helps to move you toward a better situation opens the doors for change.

REACTING RATHER THAN PLANNING

One client from the early days of my business has become, and remains, a very close friend. She was in graduate school and lived close by.

She told me the story of her life as we started working together. She moved from California to the East Coast, where she completed college and then entered the veterinarian program at Tufts University. Before she finished vet school, she met and married her husband and, within the year, became pregnant with her first child. That's when she called me. She and her husband, who was studying to be an aerospace engineer, had already consolidated two apartments into their tiny joint living space. Now with a baby on the way and a location they didn't want to leave until they both finished school, she wanted to see if they could make more space. After she finished school, they moved to Burlington, Vermont, and then had their second of two children. We stayed in touch even after their move.

When her boys were three and five years old, she and her husband decided to move back to California, where she had been born and her parents and siblings still lived. They packed up and moved quite suddenly. I never fully understood why. I knew she wanted to be close to family, but there was no initial impetus or structure for the move. Then her husband couldn't find a job in California that would help him move his career forward.

Fortunately, the company he had been working for hired him as a consultant to visit facilities in other countries and lend support in his area of expertise. He started doing a lot of international travel, working a couple of weeks in a row overseas, then flying back home for a week or two, then going off again for another two to three weeks. It was great to have her husband home with time off in California, to be with the family and their two boys, but then he was gone again for what seemed like a very long time. The situation was getting hard to bear, and they were both stressed. She said it was even affecting the kids.

Just a year and a half later they decided to move back to Vermont, where her husband could have a position, similar to his old one, that didn't require traveling as extensively. She mentioned that they were not happy in California because he was gone more than 50 percent of the time. There was some hesitation in her voice, though, because she truly loved being close to her family, and her boys had developed a strong relationship with their cousins and grandparents.

Sensing that she needed a little guidance, I said, "Trust me a little bit here; I have some experience. It seems to me that you're reacting when things aren't working out, rather than thinking about what you want. You should be working to achieve the ideal situation. What do you want? What is your goal? Do you really want to stay in California? Because if you do, you can make it work. You can find different ways."

> *Don't be pushed by your problems. Be led by your dreams.*
>
> —ANONYMOUS

Then I gave her some examples: "Think about the actresses and singers who knew what they wanted, and while struggling on their paths to fame, they didn't take no for an answer. They slept in cars; they worked until they made it happen. It's kind of the same thing for you. You need to know where you're going, so you can get there. You need to sit down with your husband, talk about it, and set goals for your family."

She said, "Who does that? Do you set family goals?"

I replied, "Yes, I do. My husband and I have a strategic planning meeting every January to develop our goals for the year. We work on his career goals and my business goals, but also goals for our marriage, each of our three kids, home improvements, financial goals, fitness, and anything else we put on the agenda. This is a great opportunity for us to get aligned on our objectives for the year. We know our goals are aligned so we are working toward the same things.

"What is your goal?" I asked her. "Ultimately, where do you see yourself in two years when you think about what makes you happy? Is it staying in Vermont; is it moving back? You need to take a step back from the madness of the situation and look at the bigger picture."

My friends were reacting to the situation rather than putting together goals and then figuring out a strategy to move them toward those goals. When they thought about the big picture, they chose to stay in Vermont, where her work as a veterinarian and his career goals were better served. They then scheduled visits with family, including destination vacations to places like Disney World, where the cousins could continue to build their bonds, and established other, less stressful ways to stay close.

DEVELOPING YOUR VISION

When Helen Keller was asked if there was anything worse than being blind, she answered, "Yes, being able to see, and having no vision."

To create an environment where you are working toward goals, you need to develop your vision, how you see yourself in the future, both in the short-term and the long-term. Think about who you want to become, in all the different aspects of your life: work, family, spiritual, fitness, romance, and so on. In the same way I encourage you to have only one calendar where you keep all your appointments, both personal and work related, your goals have to take into account your entire life, not just a portion of it. After all, every choice has consequences, and in order for your goals to be realistic, something you really believe in, you must consider the entire picture.

Think about the different aspects of your business. What do you want from a financial perspective? Is it related to the number of clients, the number of employees, or the annual profit? Do you want to develop a new product, workshop, or marketing strategy? Think about all the different aspects of your business to set your goals. The next step is to come up with specific goals for each of those aspects.

Especially for my personal goals, I need to plan with my spouse. I can't set all our goals by myself, because I don't know what his schedule is for next year and if it's going to be possible for me to do some of the things I want to do. For the children, we need to be aligned so that we schedule time and provide support for what we both think is important for raising our family. You must involve everyone who will be involved in the consequences of the goals, everyone who has a role in making them happen. They need to help you flesh out your goals and identify the tasks to be done—the actual to-dos for reaching the goal.

For your business goals, you might find it helpful to work with a strategic planning team. Even if you are a solopreneur, having a trusted team of advisers who can help you develop goals while taking an honest look at your business is a great idea. It also helps to keep you accountable.

SMART GOALS

Next, you must make sure that each goal is actionable. I like to use the SMART acronym for developing goals because SMART goals have built-in characteristics that will make achieving them possible and rewarding. Each goal should be:

- *Specific.* Each goal should be so clear that you cannot mistake what you are stating you will accomplish. This way you will have a higher chance of accomplishing it.
- *Measurable.* You need to know when you have successfully accomplished your goal.
- *Attainable.* Make sure that the specific goal and outcomes are both achievable and realistic so that you believe you can do it.
- *Relevant.* The goal needs to be something that matters to you, something that is worthwhile accomplishing.
- *Timely.* Only when you have a deadline or date for completing the goal will you be able to create a time line for accomplishing it.

Here is a simple example of a non-SMART family goal transformed into a SMART goal:

- *Goal.* Spend more quality time with my children.
- *SMART Goal.* I will spend at least fifteen minutes every night with each child reading together, starting this month.

Here is an example of how Katy turned a business goal into a SMART goal to help her achieve what was important for her to make her gym successful:

- *Goal.* Have nine hundred gym members.
- *SMART Goal.* Increase membership by 30 percent, to nine hundred members, by the end of 2013.

SMART goals will help you clarify what you need to do by when. They will help you hold yourself, and those around you, accountable for achieving the goals. Having SMART goals also allows you to perform interim analysis to assess how you are tracking against your goals throughout the year.

Having goals alone is not enough, though. As leadership expert John C. Maxwell states, "dreams don't work unless you do." It is important that the activities that you spend time on each day bring you closer to achieving your goals. This is level 4, activity-goal alignment, in the Peak Productivity Pyramid System.

After you have looked at all the different aspects of your life and developed your SMART goals, it is important to break them down into actionable steps and add them to your calendar or task management system. After all, as Antoine de Saint- Exupéry said, "A goal without a plan is just a wish." What gets planned, gets done.

In the example given previously, where your goal is to spend fifteen minutes every night reading to each child, some of the specific tasks related to that SMART goal might be:

- Eat dinner earlier so that you have more reading time.
- Leave work by a certain time so that you can make it home in time to read to the kids.
- Go to the library once a week to get new books.

Many times, I get resistance from those who don't want to have everything so planned out. These people say, "Having extensive goals takes the fun out of life."

The truth is that although having a plan is critically important, no part of it is written in stone. Life intervenes from time to time, transitions happen, priorities change, so there are many reasons that require your goals to change, too. Sometimes you might change your mind about a particular goal. Even so, to get anywhere you must start to move somewhere, in a charted direction.

Having a goal just means that you know where you're going. You can always change your mind or reassess your priorities, but you have to start somewhere. If you are going someplace and you've never been there before, you need directions, a map. Once you have that information, you can decide to take a detour and go see something beautiful you heard about on the way that you want to explore. That's fine. You are making a choice, a conscious decision. You are not just reacting and putting out fires; you're making choices.

Remember, time management is really about the choices you make. Your family and business needs will change over time. Opportunities to coach T-ball, develop a new product, or write a book don't last forever. You need to decide what is important at a given time, develop your goals, and make them happen.

SIX STEPS TO GOAL SETTING

If you've never used a SMART goals system before, here are some simple steps to get you started.

Step 1: Commit

You need to decide that you want to live a life of purpose. Establish goals that you want to achieve. You need to be able to say, "I'm committed to achieving these goals. I'm going to do it."

Step 2: Understand

Understand why it is important to have goals. If you are going to make a change, you have to understand why it is important to you. I want to have goals because I want to know where I'm going, I want to get there, live my life with purpose, do something every day that's moving me toward the bigger picture, toward what I want to be when I grow up.

Step 3: Create Goals

Set time aside to create your SMART goals. Identify others that you can work with, preferably those who can support you, hold you accountable, and whose lives your goals affect. In many cases, you will need to break your goal(s) down into smaller tasks. Even when a goal is attainable, it might be too large or complex to accomplish with a single effort.

Step 4: Break Down into Tasks

The path to achieving a goal is often a series of tasks and activities tied to that goal. You need to come up with the tasks that lead to fulfilling the goal. Maybe you are going to eat dinner earlier so that you have more time in the evening to read to your kids. Maybe you are tired of reading the same books over and over, so you're going to take your kids to the library to pick out some new ones. Maybe you are going to leave work earlier so that you have more time at home. Now you are making choices in your day that will dictate whether you reach your goal. This is taking your vision a step closer to realization—not just setting a goal, but taking action. Without identifying those activities that create family reading time, this goal is going to become a source of stress and undermine your goal of spending more quality time with your kids. Make your goals actionable by scheduling tasks to help you accomplish your goal.

Step 5: Schedule

Set a time frame. For example, "I'm going to schedule this goal at the end of the year, because business slows down in December and that will be a great time for me to act." Some people have a fiscal year ending in the middle of the year, so June might fit their time frame better. Determine the timing that works best for you, but involve anybody you need to, and then commit to following the schedule.

Step 6: Assess and Reassess

Follow up to be sure you are on track to complete your goals within your schedule. Reassess whether the SMART goal is still important to you. No goal is set in stone. Goals help you set the direction and keep you moving toward your vision.

When the vision shifts, your goals will shift. You assign new tasks and activities so that what you are doing on a daily basis aligns with your goals and your vision of who you want to become. This step is crucial for paving the way to the next and final step to the top level in the Peak Productivity Pyramid System—level 5, possibility.

First, though, there are some other important qualities that contribute to productivity to cover in the next chapter as you prepare for the top level of the Peak Productivity Pyramid.

PRODUCTIVITY POINTERS

- Align what you do each day with the goals you set in order to achieve what you want.
- Be clear about what you should and should not be doing.
- Create an environment focused on what is most important to you.
- Develop SMART goals that give you clarity and accountability.
- Break down the SMART goals into actionable tasks that help you achieve your goals.

CHAPTER 10

PAVING THE WAY TO POSSIBILITY

W orking in the world of advertising, I first discovered two of the most important attributes for living a productive life: discipline and attitude. After coming up with a packaging design proposal for the Max Factor and CoverGirl beauty lines, something I had played a key role in, my boss and I were scheduled to meet with the VP of marketing for all the Procter & Gamble brands to present our ideas.

That morning my boss got up and discovered her daughter was sick. She knew she couldn't go to the meeting and decided to send me alone. I went and presented (while my boss dialed in on the speakerphone and chimed in). The client loved the whole presentation, and I felt a huge sense of accomplishment. What made it a positive experience was being prepared, which takes discipline and having an attitude that assumed success.

So far this book has been about implementing changes in your environment and processes. It has been about all the tangible things you can do to improve your productivity. There are also some intangibles that contribute to success and increased productivity. The two most important attributes are discipline and attitude. Even if you have the best time management system set up, your life will only change if you have the discipline to implement the practices. Even if you have clear measureable goals and align your activities to achieve them, only executing those activities will accomplish your goals.

Attitude is another contributing factor. If you have a picture of your success, whatever that means to you, there is a much greater likelihood you will achieve it.

It might seem obvious, but people often get so caught up in their lives that they forget to take care of themselves. Operating under stress, being tired, and having poor nutrition diminish what you can do. It may even cloud your judgment and reduce your response time. All of these factors come under the umbrella of holistic time management, a comprehensive approach to increasing productivity. Before going into the realm of possibility, it is important to understand these less tangible aspects of productivity as well.

DISCIPLINE

My two older children have been taking karate lessons for the past two years. They go to a great school that emphasizes building character. Every month, they focus on what their instructor calls a "powerful word." Throughout the month, they do activities to explore and reinforce this word. Coincidentally, as I was writing this chapter on other factors that affect productivity, we heard that the powerful word of the month was *discipline*. In the school's newsletter, the teachers discussed ways in which we could help our children understand what discipline means.

Discipline is the bridge between goals and accomplishments.

—JIM ROHN

On one hand, we need to have discipline to follow and respect rules imposed by others. On the other hand, we must learn how to follow our own self-imposed rules. I think that the first part tends to be easier for us to follow. After all, there is a higher accountability level imposed by others.

Sometimes the challenging part of self-discipline is having enough respect for ourselves and our goals to work on them even if we don't feel like it. How often do we walk around feeling guilty about everything we should be doing that is not getting done? No matter how many tips and techniques you learn about how to become more productive, as Maya Angelou stated, "Nothing will work unless you do."

There probably isn't another quote that points out the importance of discipline more than the one by Brian Tracy in his book *No Excuses: The Power of Self-Discipline.* Tracy talks about his chance encounter with M. R. (Kop) Kopmeyer, a noted success authority, and asking him this question: "Of all the 1,000 success principles that you have discovered, which do you think is the most important?"

As Tracy writes:

[Kop] smiled at me with a twinkle in his eye, as if he had been asked this question many times, and he replied without hesitating, "The most important success principle of all was stated by Elbert Hubbard, one of the most prolific writers in American history, at the beginning of the twentieth century. He said, 'Self-discipline is the ability to do what you should do, when you should do it, whether you feel like it or not.' . . . [W]ithout self-discipline, none of them work. With self-discipline, they all work."

Thus, self-discipline is the key to personal greatness. It is the magic quality that opens all doors for you and makes everything else possible.[1]

In this one brief excerpt from *No Excuses,* three of the great men in productivity and success—Brian Tracy, Kop Kopmeyer, and Elbert Hubbard—all confirm that discipline is the most important attribute for success.

Regardless of how much you learn and no matter how many different techniques you read about, you have to have the motivation and discipline to implement and make changes.

Resources

There are countless resources available if you want to work on improving your discipline. If you do a Google search for "how to improve self-discipline," you will get more than 5 million results. Here are a few that I recommend:

The 7 Habits of Highly Effective People, by Stephen R. Covey
Peak: How Great Companies Get Their Mojo from Maslow, by Chip Conley
Mindset: The New Psychology of Success, by Carol S. Dweck, Ph.D.

ATTITUDE

Attitude is a little thing that makes a big difference.
—Winston Churchill

It has been proven that happy people are more productive. And being happy has a lot to do with your attitude. In their 2011 article in the *New York Times* called "Do Happier People Work Harder," Teresa Amabile and Steven Kramer established through their research that being unhappy at work means lower productivity. They cite one study by Gallup that estimates an annual $300 billion loss in productivity by U.S. companies as a result of people not caring for their jobs or employers. The rationale for the study was based on the concept that people who are dissatisfied show up for work less often and produce less or lower-quality work. The authors reference other research showing "that inner work life has a profound impact on workers' creativity, productivity, commitment, and collegiality. Employees are far more likely to have new ideas on days when they feel happier. Conventional wisdom suggests that pressure enhances performance; our real-time data, however, shows that workers perform better when they are happily engaged in what they do."[2]

You might feel as if there are factors impacting your negative attitude that you can't control, like a difficult boss or a job that does not give you a sense of accomplishment. Have you tried to change your attitude about it? In *The Art of Possibility*, Rosamund and Benjamin Zander talk about engaging in negative self-talk that can lead you to a downward spiral. You need to be conscious of your self-talk and change it in order to create a positive attitude.

In *The Happiness Project,* Gretchen Rubin recounts a story of a friend who worked under a challenging boss. Gretchen's friend made a rule that she wasn't going to say anything negative about her boss and that if others were saying negative things, she'd walk away. The friend turned out much happier with her job than her coworkers, and even found herself liking her boss.

Many experts recommend developing an attitude of gratitude as a way of improving your general happiness. One of the recommended methods is to keep a gratitude journal. This is a simple way of shifting your focus away from what's making you unhappy toward what makes you happy, and from what's making you feel deprived to what makes you feel fulfilled.

Resources

You are the only one who can control your attitude. Here are some recommended resources for improving your attitude:

Happiness at Work: Be Resilient, Motivated, and Successful—No Matter What, by Srikumar S. Rao, Ph.D.

The Happiness Project: Or, Why I Spent a Year Trying to Sing in the Morning, Clean My Closets, Fight Right, Read Aristotle, and Generally Have More Fun, by Gretchen Rubin

Peak: How Great Companies Get Their Mojo from Maslow, by Chip Conley

The Art of Possibility: Transforming Professional and Personal Life, by Rosamund Stone Zander and Benjamin Zander

HEALTH

While everyone knows that taking care of ourselves is important, as a culture, too many of us don't do it consistently. Everything else seems to crowd out even the most essential needs that contribute to a healthier lifestyle. We all know that if we don't feel great, we do not produce at an optimal level. A 2005 study called "Health and Productivity Among U.S. Workers" states that "labor time lost due to health reasons represents lost economic output totaling $260 billion per year."[3]

There are many factors that go into being healthy and feeling great. Everyone knows that eating well, getting enough sleep, and exercising on a regular basis will make you happier, more alert, and more productive.

A 2007 National Sleep Foundation study of more than 1,000 workers revealed that 29 percent of survey respondents fell asleep or became sleepy at work in the month prior to the survey; 12 percent of respondents reported being late for work due to sleepiness or a sleep problem.[4] Getting enough sleep at the very least will improve attendance and attentiveness at work.

Ron Goetzel and colleagues estimated that the per-employee economic burden of illness for employers averages between $300 and $400 per year for hypertension, heart disease, depression, and arthritis. Absenteeism accounts for 10 percent to 20 percent of those costs, while *presen-teeism* (showing up for work when sick but performing at a substantially reduced level of productivity) accounts for 18 percent to more than 60 percent of total costs. This means that from one-fifth to three-fifths of the total economic health costs for employers stem from on-the-job productivity losses.[5]

Making and keeping annual dental and doctor appointments is a first step toward ensuring that you know what your health risks are so that you can put preventive measures in place. Understanding how to reduce stress, create a healthy menu, and fit routine exercise into your schedule are equally important. A healthier you will mean a more productive you.

Resources

2009/2010 Staying @ Work Report, by Watson Wyatt Worldwide

Your Brain at Work: Strategies for Overcoming Distraction, Regaining Focus, and Working Smarter All Day Long, by David Rock

HOLISTIC TIME MANAGEMENT

One of my favorite time management experts, Harold Taylor, has done a lot of research on other factors that affect productivity. He subsequently developed what he calls holistic time management. He conducts tele-classes and seminars on the topic and has written a book called *Slowing Down the Speed of Life: A Holistic Approach to Time Management*. He describes his approach this way:

Holistic time management looks at the total life of the individual, as opposed to simply [the person's] environment, equipment, methods, and personal habits. Just as holistic medicine treats the whole person, so holistic time management goes beyond the quest for efficiency and effectiveness and looks at all aspects of a person's life.

. . . Holistic time management goes beyond the symptoms and traces the individual problems to their source. It treats the whole person, not just their work habits.[6]

There's more to time management than meets the eye.

—HAROLD TAYLOR

The productivity industry is moving in the direction of a holistic approach. In December 2012, I attended the Massachusetts Conference for Women, where Arianna Huffington, president and editor-in-chief of the Huffington Post Media Group, was a keynote speaker. She talked about how we can combine our professional and personal lives with less stress. She mentioned a time when she passed out from exhaustion, woke up with a broken cheekbone, and had to get stitches under her eyebrow. From that moment, she realized the ultimate key to stress reduction was sleep.

"If we don't learn to disconnect from technology and really connect with ourselves, we will become fried," Huffington said. At the *Huffington Post*, they have established nap rooms where employees are encouraged to disconnect and renew so they can be more productive.

Tony Schwartz, of The Energy Project, is another leading expert in the movement toward strategic renewal to increase productivity. In a *New York Times* column titled "Relax! You'll Be More Productive," he stated that "a new and growing body of multidisciplinary research shows that strategic renewal—including daytime workouts, short afternoon naps, longer sleep hours, more time away from the office, and longer, more frequent vacations—boost productivity, job performance, and, of course, health."[7]

You are only as strong as your weakest link. This adage is used quite frequently when analyzing staff. It can also apply to using a holistic approach for assessing individuals' productivity. You need to address all aspects of your life in order to achieve your greatest potential.

Resources

Here are some recommended resources for looking at a holistic approach to productivity:

Slowing Down the Speed of Life: A Holistic Approach to Time Management, by Harold Taylor

Be Excellent at Anything, by Tony Schwartz

While most of this book focuses on tasks and activities, this chapter has introduced areas that affect your productivity but are much harder to quantify and control. They are just as essential, though. You need to have discipline and a positive attitude to be motivated. A holistic approach will help you include the less tangible aspects of productivity in your routines, especially caring for yourself through a healthy diet, adequate sleep, and exercise. These are the intangibles that will pave the way and complete your climb to level 5—possibility.

PRODUCTIVITY POINTERS

- Look beyond the environmental and process-oriented changes you can make to improve your productivity. There are some intangible aspects of productivity that are also essential to success.
- Have the discipline to implement the changes, use the systems, and perform.
- Maintain an attitude of success to give yourself confidence and reaffirm your commitment to succeed.
- Commit to a healthy lifestyle, reducing stress, and getting enough sleep to achieve peak performance.

CHAPTER 11

LEVEL 5: POSSIBILITY

I'm not an optimist, neither am I a pessimist. I'm a very serious possibilist. It's a new category where we take emotion apart, and we just work analytically with the world.

—Hans Rosling

Named to *Time* magazine's 2012 list of the top 100 most influential people in the world, Hans Rosling defines himself as a possibilist, someone who applies statistics to characterize the human condition, allowing us to view the world, and how we affect each other's lives, in a new way. And, according to his vision, it's possible to create a world where everyone can be healthy and wealthy.

Within the context of the Peak Productivity Pyramid System, a possibilist is someone who embraces the emotion associated with change; someone who is always aware that there are new possibilities out there and always looks for the next possibility. A possibilist is constantly evolving to a new stage or state in life, always with a vision of living to full potential.

The word *possibility* brings with it feelings of hope and potential. We'll say (sometimes with great excitement), "My new house has great possibilities," or "My new employee is going to make it possible for me to do so much more!" Yet, it is much less common for us to explore the possibilities within ourselves. Level 5 of the Peak Productivity Pyramid System aims to lead you to a place where you can examine the possibilities within you. You have finally mastered the other four levels and quieted the distractions of everyday busyness. Now you are able to focus on the bigger picture. Everything else is out of the way, so you can start looking at the possibilities for your life. You, too, can become a possibilist. The great thing about possibility is that it is available for everyone.

This book talks about productivity, or the act of being productive. You have learned many different techniques to ensure that you are being efficient and effective to maximize productivity. You also know about the emotional side: maintaining discipline, having a positive attitude, and paying attention to those aspects of a healthy lifestyle that contribute to productivity. But productivity for the sake of productivity is not enough. Now that you have control over your days, over your time, you need to spend some time prioritizing to make sure that you are becoming who you want to be. If you recall, the Important/Not Urgent box (see Figure 7-1) is where the daily activities center around planning for that which is deemed important, including time spent on self-care and project work that moves you toward your goals.

You might be wondering how this level is different from the activity-goal alignment step in the Peak Productivity Pyramid. In the previous level, you worked on setting goals to give your life direction and then learned how to break those goals into actionable steps, to ensure that what you do every day is moving you closer to achieving your goals.

The possibility level is not merely about setting goals, but helping you look at your purpose. It gives you permission to dream, to pursue things that you never imagined before. It pushes you to strive for a life lived to your fullest potential.

In 2005, I worked at McKinney & Silver (now known as McKinney), an ad agency in Durham, North Carolina, that was experiencing tremendous growth at the time. To celebrate its anniversary, the agency brought in a speaker to talk about leadership. Benjamin Zander, who at the time was conductor of the Boston Philharmonic, is a gifted speaker who captivated us with his talk called "The Art of Possibility," the concept behind his book of the same title.

During the presentation, Zander told us about his practice of giving his students an A grade during the first day of class. He explained that by giving them an A, it removed the pressures of comparing themselves to each other; instead, they could think about becoming who they truly wanted to be. The only condition he imposed was requiring the students to write a letter within the first two weeks of class, dated May of next year. They had to start the letter with a simple statement, "Dear Mr. Zander, I got my A because...," and proceed to describe who they will have become by the following May to justify the A. He asked them to envision the person they *want* to become, not who they think they *should* become.

They were instructed to fall passionately in love with this person they described in their letters. Then, for the rest of the classes, Zander addressed the students as though they already were their future selves, and he noticed how this new perspective transformed their relationship. All of a sudden, the students' thinking shifted from the expectation of living up to the A to the possibility of being the person who already earned the A.

Zander's presentation and book have stuck with me throughout my career and helped shape my business and the way I work with clients. By helping people to see who they want to become, and then working with that vision of themselves (not the one they think they are now), I have watched people start to live into the person they truly want to be, quickly and with commitment.

The possibility level takes you one step further on your journey of achieving your vision of the person you will be. When you make the leap to where you want to be, instead of waiting for things to happen, you make them happen.

In his book, Zander talks about giving yourself permission to dream. Most of us are too scared to dream big because it may not happen. What happens if I fail? His response to that inevitable question is to describe three ways to face any situation in life: resignation, anger, and possibility.

He suggests that you should learn from your mistakes. Instead of putting yourself down every time you make a mistake, face failed attempts as an opportunity to learn. He goes as far as to suggest addressing your failures by using the phrase, "How fascinating!"

One very successful person who can demonstrate what that perspective has meant in her life is Oprah Winfrey. She says, "I will tell you that there have been no failures in my life. I don't want to sound like some metaphysical queen, but there have been no failures. There have been some tremendous lessons."

MASLOW AND SELF-ACTUALIZATION

Before starting the journey to possibility, let's revisit the inspiration for the Peak Productivity Pyramid System: Maslow's hierarchy of needs. At the very top of Maslow's pyramid you find self-actualization. In the original pyramid, he describes this level as such: "At the top of the hierarchy, once all of the other levels have been reasonably satisfied, is the need to become the person that we feel that we are capable of becoming. This means that we have achieved what we consider to be our very best."[1]

The parallel between Maslow's pyramid and the Peak Productivity Pyramid System became even more startling for me when I discovered the premise for promoting personal growth. In his 1968 work *Toward a Psychology of Being,* Maslow made certain points that were exactly the kind of results one could experience from possibility.

Here some of the steps that he suggests to promote personal growth that parallel the strategies and philosophy in this book: [2]

- We should teach people to be authentic; to be aware of their inner selves and to hear their inner-feeling voices.
- We should teach people that life is precious, that there is joy to be experienced in life, and if people are open to seeing the good and joyous in all kinds of situations, it makes life worth living.
- We must accept the person; we must help individuals learn their inner nature. From real knowledge of aptitudes and limitations, we can know what to build upon, what potentials are really there.
- We should teach people that controls are good, and complete abandon is bad. It takes control to improve the quality of life in all areas.
- We must teach people to be good choosers. They must be given practice in making choices, first between one goody and another.

In addition to finding these guidelines from Maslow that reinforce principles expressed by the possibility level in the Peak Productivity Pyramid System, a book called *Peak: How Great Companies Get Their Mojo from Maslow,* by Chip Conley, is about the experiences of applying the concepts behind Maslow's pyramid in today's workplace. Conley recognized that Maslow takes a positive approach to helping people realize the best they can become and adapted those attributes to corporations, helping them transform, to experience peak performance. As one example, Conley describes how employees doing even the most menial tasks learned to see possibility. These employees were shown how much their excellent job performance is appreciated and the positive effects of their efforts on those they serve.

Conley refers to Maslow's self-actualization level as transformational and says that having these peak experiences is transformational as well, something that stands out from the day-to-day, the mundane. Looking back, that day I listened to Benjamin Zander's talk on "The Art of Possibility" was a peak experience for me and certainly transformational.

The possibility level of the Peak Productivity Pyramid does not have to start with a challenge that requires you to throw out your safety net, nor does it challenge you beyond the realm of what you can visualize. Possibility is not about arriving at a final destination, but about developing an attitude of openness and awareness. It's about discovering the possibilities and then having the structure in place to help you achieve your possibility goals. When your life is in control, you can be more open to possibility along the way, which in turn will help you realize your full potential.

EARLY INFLUENCES

One of the earliest influences on me as a young girl growing up in Brazil, from a goal-setting perspective, was reading the Portuguese version of *The Cosmic Power Within You,* by Joseph Murphy. The book presents the idea that you are capable of creating your own future, your own life purpose. I was only in fifth grade at the time, but the ideas Murphy expressed had a powerful effect on me.

My mind was alive with these new ideas when our teacher, Mrs. Mead, announced that she was dividing the class into three competing groups for our next project, and at the end, after she had reviewed each of our team entries, she would tell us who won the competition. I really wanted to win, and kept thinking about it, convinced that I could control the outcome of the contest. I worked so hard. Every day at home, I remember writing down, again and again, "My team's going to win. My team's going to win." Visualizing winning, and the teacher announcing my team as the winner, were constant thoughts. I remember not sharing these thoughts with anyone, but instead, trying to motivate my team to believe in themselves.

I do think it was a tipping point in my outlook because we did win. If we hadn't, I sometimes wonder if I would have just shucked off the ideas of goal setting, believing in yourself, and the power of the mind. I might have thought, "Well, I guess that doesn't work." But instead, the experience taught me to believe in the power of your thoughts, the power of your mind, and the power of your will, which all led to goal setting and became part of who I am. In the Peak Productivity Pyramid System, I call that futuristic planning and fulfilling goals: possibility.

ALTERNATE REALITY

During my journey, I have been drawn to the studies of mental models and alternate realities. I have explored the teachings of Srikumar S. Rao, Ph.D., the author of *Are You Ready to Succeed?* and *Happiness at Work*. He has done pioneering work in motivation and helps senior executives become more engaged in work and discover deep meaning in it. One of his exercises involves creating an alternate reality.

Only when free from projections, we can be aware of reality.

—CHINESE PROVERB

For the alternate reality exercise (which you can access at Leading@ Google), Rao breaks the audience of students into small groups and has them describe, in detail, a situation that is currently of concern to them. It can be something at work or something in their personal lives. What the students don't realize is that what they are describing is not reality, it is one possible reality. That is, it's the reality they have constructed.

With the help of other students in the class, Rao then has them construct a different reality: one that is better for them and that they can get themselves to believe at some level. Then he asks his students to go out and live as if this alternate reality they have devised *is* their reality.

At first, the students are likely to come across a lot of evidence that shows that the alternate reality they have developed isn't true. But they will also see some evidence that supports the alternate reality. Rao indicates that it is important to write down any evidence that supports the alternate reality. Little by little, more supportive evidence starts to show up. This is because we see what we focus on. Rao's students are always surprised at how, over time, the alternate reality that they constructed becomes their new reality. Since the alternate reality is better for them, their quality of life improves.

Creating this alternative reality is akin to giving yourself an A for becoming the person you want to become. The experience of these teachers who encourage this behavior is evidence that by having a clear picture of the person you want to be, you have a greater likelihood of living into that reality. Here's how David Link, in his *Deviant Bits* blog, expresses this concept of going from a vision to experiencing the vision:

> The possibilist constantly imagines the seemingly impossible and pushes the boundary to see for himself what is possible. The possibilist expects opportunities everywhere, but is neither sad nor angry when an opportunity cannot be realized. Possibilists learn from failure and move on, seeking the next possibility.
>
> . . . [P]ossibilists are characterized by action. While realists sit in think tanks, possibilists sit in do tanks. Possibilists never assume that they are right. They do not deny risks or dangers. Instead, they know that every development can turn either way, good or bad. They work hard to make sure that outcomes are good.

THE FIVE E'S OF POSSIBILITY

One of the most frequently asked questions when faced with an open-ended vision of possibility is: "What is it that I really want to do or be? What is that big picture to me?" There are entire books devoted to helping people determine their life's purpose, develop life goals, create visions for a bigger purpose, and so on. Yet there are some steps you can take to start the processes for figuring out what you want to become.

> *In the measurement world, you set a goal and strive for it. In the universe of possibility, you set the context and let life unfold.*
>
> —BENJAMIN ZANDER, *The Art of Possibility*

Begin by opening yourself to the realm of possibility, and remember that it is an iterative process. Choose a bigger goal than you've ever had, then go back to break the large goal into smaller actionable goals and align your goals with activities. As you accomplish goals or as your goals change, revisit possibility to be sure you are challenging yourself to be all you can be.

How do you work toward developing possibility in your life? You can start by looking at the five E's of possibility:

1. *Enjoy*—Go back to something you used to enjoy doing but left behind.
2. *Engage*—Spend more time with people, friends, family, in your spiritual community, or in public service.
3. *Enable*—Spend more time paying attention to your health, home, and welfare.
4. *Evolve*—Spend more time and effort doing something you enjoy doing now, and take it to the next level.

5. *Explore*—Look for new challenges, something that you never dared to attempt, something that requires major changes in your outlook.

These five steps to fulfilling your possibility goals will ensure that as your productivity increases, your efforts will result in something that is more meaningful for you.

Enjoy

Return to something you used to enjoy doing, something of interest, something you were once passionate about but that's been squeezed out by other priorities. It might be the job responsibilities you most like to do, like strategic planning, or a club or hobby you once enjoyed.

A great way to regain this enjoyment is by going back and thinking about your true self, the person you are at your core. I once attended a workshop called "Sustaining a Business That Sustains You." The presenter, Irene Buchine, taught us how to look for our true selves and incorporate that part of us into our businesses, so that we can always remain passionate about what we do.

For part of a group exercise, we listed all the activities we loved as a child, such as dancing, blowing bubbles, swinging a hula hoop, reading, coloring, and so on. It was nice to be in a room full of business owners who were getting so excited about great memories. Irene showed us how that part of us becomes squashed as we grow up and have to focus on measurements, and being compared to others, with increasing responsibilities. Then she asked each one of us choose one childhood activity that we used to be passionate about and think of ways to incorporate it into our businesses.

Someone in the group, who runs a successful accounting business, chose cooking as her dormant passion. She decided to incorporate it into her business by including a recipe section in her weekly newsletter. A few months later, when we met again, she mentioned that adding the recipe column had been a huge hit with her audience because they got to know a little bit about her personality. From her perspective, she was excited about exploring new recipes to share in her newsletter. This simple exercise has at once rejuvenated her passion for cooking and created deeper relationships between her business and her clients.

This is just one way to revisit something you enjoyed doing in your past, which you can now enjoy in your present life by giving it a role in your new, more productive life of possibility.

Engage

Another area of possibility is relationships and the way we engage in community. Often, when confronted with too much to do, people sacrifice time with friends or to create friendships, time with family or to create better family relationships.

Others are at a point in life where they want to give back to others through mentoring, charitable work, or working within established organizations. Many doctors engage in volunteering. They spend vacations offering their services in Africa and other areas with too few health care resources, and they find great satisfaction in their experiences. Many organizations, like Habitat for Humanity, offer ways to give of yourself either by learning new skills on the job or placing you where you can use the talent and skills you have.

There are so many ways to become more than you are. Simply offer your time or services in caring about others; invest your time and effort to make the world a better place, whether it's in your neighborhood, local town, a nearby city, across the country, or somewhere else in the world. Perhaps you feel that you have an expanded role in the realm of spirituality and want to create goals for investing more time practicing or developing your knowledge in a particular religion or spiritual endeavor. That's valid, too. These are all examples of engaging—of going out into the larger community and either doing something you have never done before or taking on something you have done, only in a bigger way.

Enable

Look for possibility in your lifestyle. Spend more time paying attention to your health, home, and welfare. You know you will live longer and enjoy life more if you are happy and healthy. Possibility is about finding ways to incorporate healthy activities into your life, whether it's taking vegetarian cooking classes, yoga or meditation, or simply making time for sports that you love. Maybe it's as simple as taking the initiative to take charge of starting an after-work bicycle club. Two hours of bicycling can build up an appetite and burn off enough calories to enjoy a nice dinner out with friends. Maybe you've always wanted to learn a new sport, like snowboarding or windsurfing, or you are ready to meet the challenge of running a marathon. For some, losing weight can be a very fulfilling challenge to improve health. You might feel the need to improve your mental health, whether it's learning relaxation techniques or working with a therapist to get rid of self-limiting behaviors.

Another aspect of enabling a more fulfilled you is your external environment. They say that most home improvements take place within the first year of ownership. Anything past that time often goes on a perpetual to-do list, as do repairs and needed upkeep. A goal of possibility can be remodeling, redecorating, or just accomplishing those finishing touches languishing on that list. You might have the dream of designing a different living situation. Perhaps it's upgrading to a new home that's larger, or perhaps downsizing to one that is smaller. A new living location can afford new possibilities. How about an ocean view with a harbor for a sailboat or a condo with no maintenance on a golf course? You might want to move from the city to the country, or vice versa. What living situation creates the sense of satisfaction or achievement you need in order to fulfill your picture of the person you want to be?

Pave the way for a change of surroundings. It will enable the possibility for you to live a happier, healthier life.

Evolve

Spend more time and effort doing something you enjoy doing now. One of the easiest exercises is to identify what is possible within all the tasks, activities, roles, and responsibilities you have right now. You can look at what you love to do the most, what gets you excited, keeps you interested, or is an always-welcome experience. How can you incorporate more of that into your life, move more of it into your Important/Not Urgent box?

If you love your leadership role but have few opportunities to lead, where could you go or what could you do to create more opportunities?

If you love to teach, develop long-range plans, create clever graphics, write, brainstorm, the list goes on. You can find ways to increase the possibilities of using those skills that you already have and love to use the most.

Explore

Explore what's possible for your life. What is your purpose? Exploring is about what you haven't done yet. It's about opening ways to stretch yourself and your abilities further than you ever thought possible. Maybe you've never liked your career choice and want to find a way to have a more fulfilling job. Maybe you haven't had time to think about starting a family, but that is part of the reality you would like to see for your life.

When living within the realm of possibility, Zander suggests that to create goals you start off by asking:

What if?
How about?
What's next?

Unless you make time to think about what-if and what's next, you might never set the goals to make something new or different happen. Remember, possibility is about *making things happen* for you, rather than waiting for them to happen to you.

POSSIBILITY GOALS IN MIND

Another example of realizing a possibility goal is how this book came about. For more than a year, I had been thinking about writing a book. With so many ideas, I needed to get them out of my head and organized somehow. I wrote my thoughts into a single document, including a number of pages with detailed notes about what would be in it. But I knew I couldn't invest the time to sit down and write a book. There was no way. In addition to my business commitments, my children were very young and depended on me for so much. My thought was, "I'm going to do it someday; that is definitely part of my goals, but it's at the very top of the pyramid and a very long-term goal."

One day, I went into Starbucks with my children to get some hot chocolate as a reward for something they had done. We were sitting there having our hot chocolate, and there was a man at the table right next to us working on his laptop. During a brief lull in the kids' continuous prattle, he remarked, "Your kids are so cute. I've been watching them since you came in, interacting with each other, you, and everything around them."

We started a conversation. He asked what I did; then I asked what he did. He said, "I'm a writer."

"Oh, I'm so sorry we're here. The last thing you need is three kids making so much noise while you are trying to write," I said apologetically.

"No, I love kids," he replied.

So I asked, "What kind of writing do you do?"

He talked about a novel he had cowritten. Then he described how he had written a business book for a motivational speaker as a ghostwriter. Up until then I had never considered the possibility of using a ghostwriter. That conversation opened up a whole new possibility, a new way to explore writing the book with a more manageable time investment.

Not long after, I was sitting with a trusted friend who had completed a book, so I asked her, "Tell me. How did you go about writing your book? What was the process like?"

She described how she had help writing her book and talked about the person she had worked with—who is the person I eventually worked with as well.

Once the possibility of writing a book opened in my life, I found opportunities—there were new prospects for how to write my book, and ultimately, the opportunity to actually write it. Once you have the goal, then you can see opportunities that present themselves for you to fulfill the goal.

Possibility is the top of the pyramid because, if you are drowning in chaos, feeling completely out of control, you are not going to recognize opportunities that present themselves. Why? First, because you probably don't even have any goals, so you don't know what you want. Second, because you are going to be too busy just trying to breathe. Only when you are at the level where you have goals and everything else is in order can you open yourself to possibilities. Once you put thought into what possibilities would be the most meaningful, you will recognize opportunities that come up and be open to those possibilities.

Now that you have explored different ways to live to your fullest potential, it is time to engage in your vision and make it a reality. Start living every day with that new reality in mind. Start envisioning your success, whether it's by using Srikumar Rao's alternate reality exercise, Benjamin Zander's "give yourself an A" technique, or some other method. Fall passionately in love with this new vision, and start living every day as if it is your new reality.

Bringing together all the productivity strategies you've learned so far, and implementing them in your office environment, brings us to the creation of a power office, which is our next chapter.

PRODUCTIVITY POINTERS

- Climb the steps of the Peak Productivity Pyramid and it leads to the life-changing realm of possibility.
- Take advantage of your improved productivity to do more of what will fulfill you.
- Dream and explore ways to live up to your full potential.
- Realign your goals and activities as needed to achieve your full potential.

CHAPTER 12

POWER OFFICE

I f you are looking for ways to be sure you continue to thrive in your own business or remain competitive in the workforce, then what you have read so far in this book will set you up for success. Now that you've learned about the five steps in the Peak Productivity Pyramid System, this chapter will review much of that information and show you how to apply these strategies in a new way: to create the power office.

Among the reasons mentioned by a Small Business Administration study for new businesses failing, productivity is clearly high on the list, and more specifically, procrastination and poor time management. It is rarely about a lack of skill in your career or passion for your area of interest. So often when you are working either on your business or career and trying to get things done day in and day out, it is easy to forget to take a step back and look at how your business or your offices are set up for success. Beyond the systems you've explored in this book, an additional way to increase your productivity is by choosing to create a power office. It's not about the business-specific operations, so this one strategy applies to anyone who has an office.

By establishing a power office, you can be more efficient and effective. *Efficient* and *effective* are terms that are used interchangeably in management and business, but their definitions are very different. In his article "Efficiency vs. Effectiveness," Harold Taylor defines them as such:

> The most frequently cited differentiation is that efficiency is doing something in the best possible way, while effectiveness is doing the best possible thing.
>
> There are many ways to express this difference: Efficient means you are doing things right, and effective means you are doing the right things. When you are working efficiently, you are completing tasks in the best possible way, and when you're working effectively, you are concentrating your efforts on the best possible tasks. However you express it, when you get organized and productive and work both efficiently and effectively, you start approaching excellence.[1]

The power office is an environment that sets you up to be efficient so that you can be effective.

Before you start creating your power office, it helps to look at and analyze your current space to understand what's working and what's not. Usually you have a pretty good idea if something isn't working, but it is not always easy to know how to fix it. Even when you know how to fix something, sometimes it's hard to make the change. We know that the piles of paper we see aren't working well for us. Neither are the e-mails popping up as a frequent distraction. Why should you change? Why does it matter? Everyone is going to have a different answer, but in order to make change happen and implement some of the ideas for a power office, it will take some time. I like to think of this as a time investment.

Often, with clients, the first thing I hear is, "Oh, I don't have time to get organized. I don't have time to change. I can't do it." Our natural tendency and first reaction is to resist change. In order to take that step and make a change, it is critical to understand why doing something differently matters, as well as the positive effects that difference will have as a return on our time investment. It takes time to make more time. Yes, it is going to take time up front, but it's an investment that will save you so much later on.

What's the value of setting up a power office? Maybe it's being able to walk into your office and start being productive within a couple of minutes or less. Maybe you want to feel more relaxed in your office or more productive. Whatever your reason is, it's important that you identify that before you start making changes.

How do you feel in your office?

I have seen offices that were so cluttered you couldn't see the floor. One client I worked with had a home office that was so messy she never worked there (see Figure 12-1). Just walking into that space, she felt

Figure 12-1. Office clutter. *Author's photo.*

extremely overwhelmed and stressed out. Rather than energized, she felt drained. In order to work, she drove to Starbucks, a place that can hardly be considered relaxing. There is constant noise from loud espresso machines, people talking, dishes clashing, and distracting movements, with customers milling around, coming, and going. It's not a place for focusing on work, yet it was a better environment than her own office.

She is not alone. I worked with an interior designer who also had a home office. Her house was absolutely gorgeous. All the rooms were decorated and beautiful, but her home office was always closed. Nobody ever saw it. That room was the only one in her house that she absolutely dreaded having to enter because it was so cluttered. So, instead of working there, she traveled around the house with her laptop working in the kitchen, at the dining room, in the living room, or wherever else she found herself. She only opened the office door to throw things in, then quickly shut it. How do you feel in your office? You should feel powerful. What does power mean to you in relationship to your office or work environment?

Through the years, some of the people I've worked with have defined power as being in control. Others say it's being in command of knowing where and how to access everything easily and quickly, and focusing on the task at hand. Others say it's about feeling respected, whether in person or speaking on the phone, by both your peers and customers. Power can also mean you inspire your employees and others to have confidence in you. Having a power office is the culmination of what you have learned along the way, climbing the Peak Productivity Pyramid steps.

You want to feel inspired, productive, and powerful in your office. There are five primary characteristics for achieving an office space that allows you to operate from a position of power:

1. Create organized and defined work areas.
2. Implement streamlined processes and systems.
3. Work on planned tasks and activities that align with your goals.

4. Operate from the power position.

5. Surround yourself with a future vision.

ORGANIZE YOUR WORK AREAS

We know that having piles of papers covering a desk can have a negative impact on your career. Studies show that bosses are less likely to promote someone who has a disorganized or messy workspace. Statistics also indicate that if you have disorganized work areas, you may not have that feeling of power that we define as being respected, inspiring confidence, and simply being able to find things.

When you organize your work areas, your surfaces are uncluttered and items that you use every day are easily accessible. You have a separate system for future tasks and activities so that your work area helps you focus on your current tasks. This setup allows you to achieve a natural flow of work through your desk or office. Creating a flow of future, current, and past work ensures that nothing gets stuck in piles, which reduces clutter.

Having a power office will empower you. More important, you will have a work space that will help you be more productive and reflect a positive image.

Uncluttered Surfaces

The removal of clutter enhances your ability to focus. Think about a pile of papers that is currently sitting on your work space. How does it make you feel? Chances are that the clutter represents a symbolic clue of where you're stuck in your career. Removing the clutter from your space will invite new opportunities. Once you start making changes to your environment, you will start to feel more empowered, which will impact other facets of your career. An organized office with uncluttered surfaces enhances creativity and discipline and enables you to make decisions.

Designated Areas

How do you create organized work areas? If you have ever visited a kindergarten classroom, you may have noticed that they are typically organized into clearly defined spaces that are focused on specific activities. There is usually a reading area, a space for arts and crafts, and so on. It is clear to see that the room has different zones for different activities that take place in the classroom. You can apply that same model to your office.

Think about creating different zones for the different activities that you do in your office. The desk is your zone for working on your laptop and current projects, sorting mail, filing, and making phone calls. You'll want to have a filing system and paper shredder close to where you handle your incoming mail and other papers. If you spend time on research, staying current in your field, or reviewing proposals, you might want a separate, more comfortable area for your reading activities. You could cluster a few chairs with a little table for meetings that happen in your office.

Pay attention to the different activities that occur in your typical day or week. Determine what supplies, implements, and furniture you will need at hand to conduct them, with everything organized in those specific areas. Only include those items you need to support your current activities, and have them readily available. This one strategy will encourage you to focus on your current activities without distractions.

Backup Systems and Storage

If you only have on hand what you need for your immediate activities, that means you will need a system for backup items, such as extra office supplies and reference files that you don't need to access very often. Perhaps there is a storage closet located in a central area. If you have a home office, consider carving out some room in your basement or your attic.

Maybe you have a couple of shelves high up on a bookshelf. There's always a way to make it work. You don't necessarily have to spend money to buy furniture or containers. By making a conscious decision about where you are going to store things and putting these backup items somewhere less accessible, you free up space within your immediate work areas.

Work Area Efficiency

Another aspect of the organized work space is having a big solid desk with a large surface for work, and at least one, if not two, filing drawers to keep your active files nearby. The desk should also have drawers for your supplies, so they are easily accessible and organized. You should also have a large chair that spins and rolls, helping you access what you need. Perhaps you can roll back to open a filing cabinet that's behind you.

Take time to think about what files you want immediately accessible, which ones you will reference less frequently but fairly often, and then those you'll need infrequently, if at all. In an ideal situation, you will have a file drawer or two in your desk with your current and active projects and papers that you need to access. Behind you, place a larger filing cabinet with reference materials that you don't need to access all the time. Keep your storage files in a more remote location. Create a work area where you will be able to access what you need to work efficiently while you're sitting on your chair.

Tip: If multiple people use your office and your desk space, consider using labels to keep things organized. Having space in your drawers labeled to show where supplies belong will help everybody put them back in the right place.

You also have to think about bookshelf space as an element of an organized office. That's often overlooked when people are setting up their offices. They don't always think about bookshelf space, and most of us have several books and reference items that we like to keep around when we conduct our businesses. You will want a place to put those items.

In the chapter on eliminating clutter, we talked about the different options for managing your papers. This is the time to think about whether the systems you have are working for you.

Folder Systems and Files

The last element of an organized work area is to create a well-thought-out file system. Most of us have a difficult time with paper. Even most professional organizers don't love handling paper; it's not fun. We all handle a lot of papers and they just keep coming. It is not something you can just do once and be finished. It's like laundry; you have to keep doing it. So it is important to have a clear system for handling your papers.

Because most of us have entered the workforce in an established company, our experience with filing comes from inherited systems that someone else set up. Those systems are usually kept in filing cabinets, so that's how we think it needs to be done. If you have inherited cabinets that are empty and remain so, or files in your cabinets are five or more years old and you have never opened the drawer, it's probably because that system is not the best for you. This is the time to consider other solutions, such as binders, especially if your system will be based on categories. I used binders when I worked in advertising. We had one binder per client. We had client meetings all the time, and it was much easier to carry all the history organized chronologically in the binder. It was easy to access and show items during our discussions. That was a great solution for that business.

There are other options discussed in the chapter on physical organization, such as magazine boxes on a shelf, decorative boxes, or a vertical filing organizer. I think most of us will still use a filing cabinet at least for some reference files, but you don't have to use just that storage system all the time. You might want to have multiple types of filing systems depending on the type of information, how you use it, and how often you need access.

As an example, on my desk in my home office, I have two drawers, and I use them for different categories of my business. One is for clients; one is for reference materials for classrooms and other presentations. All the other papers go in a separate filing cabinet. I also have an active project filing system on my desk. It doesn't matter what system you choose. It is not about the system itself, but about the conscious decision of how you are going to use it.

Paper lying in piles in plain view is usually a symptom of someone having no trustworthy filing system. The papers pile up because we want to remember to do what's required on each paper. Once you find a system you trust, the stacks will be temporary and under control. You need to make a conscious decision to take action to deal with your incoming papers systematically and on an ongoing basis. You want a system where you touch everything once and you can decide immediately what to do with each paper. You can use the Three To's of sorting (to do, to keep, to toss) described in the chapter on getting rid of physical clutter. You can use another system, but be sure it is simple and helps you make a decision instantly about each piece of paper as you handle it—whether to keep it, do something with it, or toss it away (recycle or shred).

Research says it usually takes about twenty-one days to break a habit and form a new one. Once you decide what the best system is and you implement the changes, set up at least a weekly maintenance schedule. Once a week, maybe on Friday afternoons, or whatever day fits into your schedule, set up time to routinely maintain your new system. If you notice that piles of papers are still accumulating, something is not working. By setting aside time to focus on implementing your system, you can analyze what's working and what's not. You can then change or adapt to have a system that works for you. The key is to make a conscious decision, knowing what you like and what you don't. Once you have been using a system that works for a long time, it will become second nature.

You'll just do it. You want to have processes and systems in place that are streamlined, especially as your business grows.

STREAMLINE PROCESSES AND SYSTEMS

Well-defined job descriptions, policies and procedures, and operation manuals for essential functions, such as sales and human resources (HR), are familiar to those of you who work in bigger companies. However, some smaller businesses that are growing and expanding and hiring new employees may not have created these processes. Small companies grow and at first don't need these specifications. Everyone knows what everyone else does. They pitch in to do what's needed. They have never even thought of having job descriptions, HR policies, or other procedures. It is easiest to start developing these procedures from the very beginning, of course, but once a company reaches a size where the lack of procedures creates inefficiencies, it's critical. Even for larger companies, as your business grows and expands, how will your systems accommodate that growth and change? When you hire new employees, you want to think about how your processes and systems will be used by them and streamline your processes for everyone.

You also want to think about delegation. You want to have systems in place that make delegation easier, because you have to think about where you can use your time most effectively. Delegation gives you the best return on your time investment, and is also great for training and empowering your employees.

Having these systems in place makes the routine process of running and operating within a company more efficient.

PLAN AND ALIGN GOALS AND ACTIVITIES

You shouldn't need to spend much time each day deciding what your objectives are and what tasks and activities you will work on. You also want to minimize working on things that do not contribute to achieving your goals. You want to be certain that you are being as effective as possible in what you do. Being able to do that starts with strategic planning.

You can only create an environment where you are working effectively, working on the most important tasks, if you know your big-picture strategy. Where you want to be, who do you want to become? Streamlined planning is knowing what tasks and activities will ensure that you are being effective as you achieve your goals. One of the most important aspects of implementing a power office is having a strategic plan. Even if we create one, often we forget to revisit the plan because we become busy. In a big company, sometimes a strategic plan and the company's goals don't necessarily trickle down to the employee level. Take a look at business goals, and then set individual goals that directly relate to the company goals, whether that's in a company you own or one you work for.

I frequently work with executives within large corporations who don't measure each employee's performance against company goals. Setting up review processes that directly relate to goals is one of the most significant changes needed to create a more productive environment. Just as important as setting goals is identifying the tasks and activities that will achieve those goals.

Plan Tasks

Having a strategic plan will not tell you what to work on each day. You need to break those goals into tasks and activities. You need to have a list of everything you think you need to do. Just like physical clutter and electronic clutter, you can have brain clutter; so many thoughts swirling around in your head with no order or structure. Nearly every productivity system will tell you to do a brain dump—get every action item out of your head and recorded somewhere else. Then follow the three P's of time management: plan, prioritize, and perform. That will help you make your to-do list and schedule activities in your calendar. Look at each one of the tasks and weigh it against the urgent/important grid (described in Chapter 7, on prioritizing your time) or any other system that helps you align your activities to your goals.

Things that are urgent keep popping up and demand immediate attention, so we spend too much time in our lives putting out fires. At the end of the day, we feel as if we haven't accomplished anything, even though exhaustion tells us we were very busy. We responded to 250 e-mails, went to meetings, answered phone calls. But did we do anything to move us toward our goals?

I had a client who worked in event planning, which is a deadline-driven business. All day long, her boss (who was always very stressed out) called her to talk about things that were coming up right away. While she was trying to work on an event, her boss constantly interrupted her. She was so frustrated. She began to use one little, tiny trick about setting expectations. She talked to her boss, explaining her frustration, and then suggested, "If you need to reach me urgently, call. If not, send me an e-mail. I'll check my e-mail every two hours, and I'll respond then." Making that one change in their communication ground rules freed up her time significantly.

It's one thing to have a plan and another to stick to it. Once you align your activities with your goals, look at how you are spending your day. What distractions, interruptions, or unnecessary tasks interfere with your routine? What happens that seems to be counterproductive to achieving your goals? Look at how you can change your environment by minimizing distractions and unproductive tasks. Sometimes it's just a conversation and setting up expectations. Other times it might require changes in your job description or delegating.

Two hours out of every workday is wasted due to interruptions, and they come in many forms. Many times it's self-imposed obstructions: going online, checking e-mail, Facebook, all sorts of things that we do. There are also external interruptions: people walking in, calling. You want to try to prevent these interruptions. If you're doing work that is moving you forward toward your goals, you need concentrated effort. Shut off your phone, shut off your e-mail, and make sure you have some time when you are focused on your work. Do what you need to protect that time.

Schedule Activities

The secret is not to prioritize your schedule, but to schedule your priorities.

—Stephen Covey

You want to have tasks and activities that are planned. You want to not only have a to-do list, but you want to have those activities scheduled to allow time for getting them done. The planned activities will be different for everyone, depending on your role and type of business. A weekly staff meeting is a great way to know that you will see your staff, say, every Monday, so you won't spend your whole week e-mailing them to set up the meeting. Staff meetings streamline communication with employees. You can keep a list of everything you need to address so that you don't have to chase people down during the week. You can set up a weekly structure for any other repeating tasks so that you are not worried about when you're going to get to do them. If you know you have some things that happen daily, weekly, monthly, or annually, why not schedule them into your routine?

For example, if you say, "I'm going to pay bills every fifteenth and thirtieth of the month," and schedule time in your calendar or use a reminder, then all of a sudden, those swirling thoughts in your mind about forgetting, being late, or paying penalties are gone. You know the time on your calendar or reminder task list will pop up to prompt you to fulfill your commitment to pay your bills. That will free you to think of other, more important thoughts.

Another example of streamlining planned activities is to have a companywide calendar where everyone can see each other's schedules. That minimizes wasted time on scheduling.

Create a weekly structure for recurring tasks. Failing to plan is planning to fail. A lot of people resist the basic weekly structure because they don't want to feel as though every second of every day is planned. The truth is, when you have a plan, you can always break the plan if you have a crisis or if something more important comes up. When you have a plan, you are making a conscious decision to do one thing over another; you are deciding based on priorities.

One of the most challenging planned activities can be checking e-mail.

Manage E-Mail

You know that e-mail can be a huge time consumer, so be sure to implement an e-mail management strategy of your choosing or else use the A, B, C's method introduced in the chapter on electronic organization: access, batch, check, delete, execute, and file.

Also, schedule how frequently you check your e-mail. Rather than leaving e-mail always on, schedule specific times of the day—say, four times a day—that you will devote to applying the A, B, and C's. If you are used to checking e-mail all the time, you might want to start with looking hourly, and then reducing the frequency a little bit at a time until you reach four times or fewer in a day.

OPERATE FROM THE POWER POSITION

Feng shui is a Chinese-based practice of arranging things to create a positive flow of energy. Not everybody believes in this energy flow idea, but I encourage you to use the tips because the principles of feng shui and productivity have a great deal of overlap. For example, feng shui believes that clutter creates stagnant energy and blocks energy flow. Professional organizers believe in decluttering to increase productivity and reduce stress. While I'm not a feng shui expert, I have learned from workshops, searching the Web, and reading books that feng shui will help you set up your office in a way that inspires greater productivity and confidence. Here are the basics for the power office.

* *Situate your desk in the power position.* The position of your desk is one of the most important adjustments you can make to your office. By placing your desk in what's called the command position, you are asserting yourself as a powerful and successful creator of your life. The command position is located diagonally across from and facing the door or room opening. You also want it situated so that your chair back is against wall space rather than a window or other opening. Figure 12-2 shows the three correct ways to place your desk to establish this position of power. Ideally, you want a clear path of vision from the door to your desk, as this establishes an even greater sense of authority. This position is also considered the lucky corridor of any room, so you definitely want to have your desk there.
* *Sit behind a power desk in a power chair.* Your desk should be of solid construction with a lot of surface area and easy access to drawers for your files and supplies. A power chair has a high back and armrests. Ideally, the high back would be solid construction, but it doesn't have to be. Also, if you can't position your desk so that the chair back isn't against a window, a high back chair is enough.

Try it. Set up a high back chair, against the wall, behind a power desk, in a power position. See if you feel a greater sense of energy and

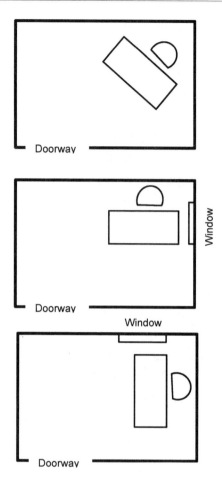

Figure 12-2. Power position.

power while you work. Pay attention to how others entering your office react as a result. Will it be the same or different?

POSSIBILITY FOR THE POWER OFFICE

The top level of the pyramid is possibility. Once you do the things at the first four levels—getting organized, setting up systems, aligning your goals to your daily work—you should consider the top step in the Peak Productivity Pyramid System: possibility.

Most office decor is devoted to current priorities and past achievements, such as family photos, awards, and diplomas. A critical element that is often overlooked is incorporating items that remind you of your career goals. A power office should include reminders of things that inspire you and are aligned with your career aspirations.

When I introduce this concept in a workshop, I ask people to close their eyes and envision one goal they have for their business or career. Having a few items that remind you of a future vision will keep you focused and motivated. This one simple tactic can help you focus on your future accomplishments, rather than your past ones. Take the time to write down one of your future goals. Now brainstorm an artifact that symbolizes that goal for you. It could be a picture of that beach house or boat that you want to buy, a picture of someone you admire, or a piece of art that symbolizes that achievement, such as a positive upward spiral or breaking the glass ceiling.

Everything in your power office should inspire you and serve as a reminder of your goals and your vision.

Time is the greatest nonrenewable resource we have. We can always make more money, work more days, but we can never get time back once we've wasted it. It's important to make the right choices in order to achieve success, to use our time effectively and efficiently. Apply what you've learned and set up your power office so that when you walk in, you can be productive, energized, and feel powerful in your space.

Not everyone has the skills or the time to figure out for themselves how to apply these lessons. You might find that hiring an expert to lead you through the steps to increased productivity will get you started on the path to possibility faster.

PRODUCTIVITY POINTERS

- Create a productive environment that supports your systems and goals.
- Create a high-energy physical space so that you operate from a position of power.
- Create a workplace designed for efficiency.
- Create a power office.

CHAPTER 13

HIRING A PRODUCTIVITY CONSULTANT

Y ou've bought this book; you are committed to improving your productivity. Reading this chapter title, though, you are probably asking, "Shouldn't I be able to do it myself?" After all, as you've read all along, the simpler the system, the better. It is not rocket science. Nearly every successful businessperson implements assorted systems to improve productivity. It's not some crazy specialization only a few highly trained individuals are privy to.

If you try to do it yourself and find that you're less than satisfied with the results, the fault may not be in the systems you are using or the advice you learned in your reading. It could be a question of accountability, or having an honest outside perspective. Perhaps you need someone who can understand the difficulty you have adapting or adhering to a new system.

Even if you know how to plan a menu and eat a healthy diet, it's not always easy to follow the diet. You know it's important to incorporate an exercise regimen into your week and get enough rest. We all know what we should do to stay healthy, but we don't always do it. Sometimes we need someone to tailor a program to our special needs so that we don't overdo it, take on too much, and change too quickly or too little.

People who don't see progress tend to get discouraged. Sometimes all you need is an accountability partner—someone who is going to follow up and ask about your progress and how you feel about the changes. Having someone who is motivational to cheer you on might be just what you need to keep you on track.

Sometimes having somebody come in with an outside perspective can help you to see hurdles that you are unaware of and that are impeding your progress. A consultant who understands your business and how you're tackling your day-to-day tasks and activities will have a fresh take on your situation. With the right experience, a productivity professional can shorten the time from wanting to improve to making the changes that increase your productivity. While most people can make productivity changes and improve the quality of their life by reading a book, for many others, working with a consultant who has that outside perspective can lead to major life changes.

Nearly everyone knows what a personal trainer does. Hiring a personal trainer means paying someone to create a fitness program just for you. Trainers assess your current abilities; they ask you questions about your health, needs, and goals; and then they put together a program to help you achieve your goals. Hiring a productivity consultant should work the same way. If you decide to hire someone, however, be informed and be sure to hire the right person.

HIRING ATTRIBUTES

When you hire someone to help you become more productive, you want someone who goes about it logically, methodically, and with a clear focus on you and your needs. Here are the twelve essential attributes you should look for in a productivity consultant.

Attribute 1: Empathy

Empathy is very important. You need someone you are immediately comfortable with and feel you can trust. Productivity consultants get to know their clients personally and professionally. To help the client effectively, they will need to know a lot of personal information. The more you can trust the consultant, the more quickly you'll open up, and the more you'll be willing to reveal. With better insight, the easier it will be for the consultant to help you move more quickly to a productive life that helps you achieve your goals.

When you feel the consultant is judging you, the normal reaction is to try and defend yourself rather than reveal vulnerabilities or problems. When you don't feel the real motivation is to help you, but instead to make you reliant on coaching until the next session, or even to keep the payments coming, you can't have an empathic relationship. If you feel the consultant is trying to impress you rather than help you, that is another sign that the relationship will not be as productive as it should be. You need to have a relationship of trust, which comes only when you feel that the consultant's true intentions are to help you.

Attribute 2: Honesty

While it's important that your consultant be nonjudgmental, another aspect of that is honesty. There are ways of being honest and straightforward without making a client feel scolded, reprimanded, belittled, or any one of the many words that ultimately make a person feel judged rather than coached or guided. You need honesty to make progress without wasting time.

Attribute 3: Assessing

Once you feel comfortable with someone and know the productivity consultant can be honest with you, assessment is the next most important phase of launching any project. If consultants assess incorrectly or misdiagnose the client's needs, they are going to spend a lot of time and effort trying to fix something that may not be broken. Getting started in the right direction is what makes the consultant, the client, and ultimately the relationship successful. Be sure your consultant uses an assessment that helps guide you through a thorough understanding of your strengths and weaknesses.

Attribute 4: Questioning

When hiring a consultant, you want someone who asks a lot of questions. Generally, when we hire someone to help us do something, it's because we don't fully understand what we want and need. Even when people might think they know what they want, often they don't know what they need. We need to rely on the consultant to help us understand what is best for us. Consultants are able to uncover what we need by asking questions and drilling down until the answer is obvious, so their recommendations make sense. Someone who asks questions about your current practices, your preferences, and your visions for the outcome is more likely to get to your core needs and desires. That's where goals and objectives can be created.

Attribute 5: A Good Listener

Asking questions is the basis, but even more important is someone who is listening more than talking. The Productivity Pyramid Assessment found in Chapter 2 is an excellent starting point for asking questions.

Good consultants, however, ask more probing questions depending on the client's answers. Probing questions only happen when a consultant listens to a client's responses, then asks another question, listens, and asks another, until the consultant is satisfied that the answers are honest, revealing the client's true desires, root problems, or hidden agenda. Listening leads a consultant to the best path for achieving the right goals.

Attribute 6: Experienced

Look for consultants who have worked with many different types of clients. Look for someone who has broad experience or, conversely, someone specializing in your specific area of business who has a depth of experience. Either one is fine: Breadth of experience is a lot of diverse experience; depth of experience is a highly specialized niche.

Because everyone thinks differently and different people process information their own way, consultants who have worked with a variety of clients will have that broad experience to draw upon to help you with a specific problem. They've experimented to find the right solution for the person who has procrastination and clutter issues, the person who feels the need to connect to e-mail constantly and has a million interruptions a day. They will be able to drill down to a solution that fits your circumstances more quickly, gauge the rate of improvement, and recommend course corrections along the way.

On the other hand, hiring someone who specializes in your specific area of business or expertise, and has a depth of experience in your niche, has benefits as well. These consultants can draw from their past experiences to help you in the context of your industry, position, or profession because they will understand the specific demands, the calendar or recurring events, the most common problems and solutions in your field. The main point is to hire someone with experience, but someone who can adapt to your specific needs.

Attribute 7: Specific to Your Needs

Be careful that the consultant isn't steering your conversation, leading you to agree with a set program, a one-size-fits-all prescriptive remedy. Good consultants will not have their own agenda or come to the meeting trying to impose their own system. A well-run assessment flows in a way that is more like a natural conversation. That's because good consultants are listening carefully to your answers and reflecting on what you are saying, so you know they understand where you are and where you want to be. A productivity consultant should create an individualized program, with achievable time frames to fit your needs, goals, and objectives. You should be able to get a sense of the consultant's ability to do that in your initial interviews.

Attribute 8: Well Versed in Different Systems

Avoid anyone who comes with an agenda and who is interested in imposing a specific system. Rather, you want to seek out consultants who are knowledgeable about several different systems and who can work with clients to identify the best system to help meet their goals and solve their unique problems. You should never feel pushed into one system without hearing about alternatives. Consultants should give you options beyond the systems they promote and habitually use. One size does not fit all.

Attribute 9: Flexible

Avoid working with someone who tries to fix something that is working, something that isn't broken. It is also important to know how to adapt what is working into a new system or combination of systems. Not everything needs to be fixed. If something is working well, but perhaps hindering other aspects of productivity, you want someone who can find creative solutions to adapt what's working and integrate it with any new system or systems you are implementing. That's another reason for hiring someone skilled in using an assessment and in questioning and listening techniques to find out what *is* working for the client.

Attribute 10: Simplifying

You will want to work with someone who can break things down in a way that's easy to understand and easy to implement. The simpler the action steps, the simpler the to-dos and the homework, the more successful the client will be implementing the recommended ideas and techniques. Achieving success also creates a healthier, more productive relationship.

Avoid the consultant who tries to impress you by using jargon or difficult words, because in truth, productivity or time management is not rocket science. It is all about using simple techniques. They may be new skills that you haven't been introduced to yet, or maybe you just need a reminder about a technique you've learned before but have forgotten about because you haven't needed it until now. Nothing about these systems is super-complicated, so avoid the consultant who overcomplicates things. The better a consultant is at breaking things down, the easier the client will find it to be successful implementing new techniques.

Attribute 11: Clear Business Policies

It's important for the consultant to be up front about pricing, along with defining the scope of work and services you will receive. You will want to have a contract to review so that you have clear expectations about the duration and scope of work, along with your commitments and theirs. Work only with someone who uses a contract. Be sure all the terms are clear. People who use complicated language in their contracts are going to lean toward more complicated language in everything else. A contract should be clear and easy to understand, so you can make a decision about whether the services meet your needs.

If you think the prices are too high, the commitments too low, remember you can negotiate. Avoid contracts that lock you into a long-term commitment. You should be able to adapt the frequency and duration of your sessions as your needs change. Sometimes consultants will give you a fifteen- to thirty-minute consultation for free to demonstrate their abilities and style.

Attribute 12: Professional

Professionalism conjures up a myriad of images, both in terms of behavior and presence. Ultimately, you want to work with someone you could recommend to your associates, even your own clients. Dress, grooming, attitude, and manners all go into deciding whether this person will fit in with your work environment. If an associate or even a customer drops in, will you feel comfortable introducing this person? Is this a person you would refer to them? Punctuality, reliability, stick-to-itiveness, confidence, and all the other adjectives that define professionalism are important characteristics to review before hiring a productivity consultant.

INTERVIEW QUESTIONS TO ASK

The twelve attributes you want in a consultant can lead to a more satisfying and successful relationship to help you on your way to greater productivity. Knowing what attributes are important is one thing; determining how well your candidates embody them is another.

To find out whether your candidates have these attributes, you need a list of questions that will help you find the right match for your needs.

Here are some examples of questions that might help you when interviewing a productivity consultant:

1. How long have you been in business?
2. Do you belong to any professional associations?
3. Are you certified?
4. Have you worked with any clients in my industry before?
5. What is your client retention rate?
6. How long do you typically work with a client before they reach their goals?
7. After the goal is reached, do you provide some kind of maintenance work or check-in schedule?
8. What are your hours?
9. How flexible is your schedule?
10. Do you consult over the phone, as well as in person?
11. What kind of systems do you use the most with clients?
12. Do you have other systems that you've used?
13. Would you say you have a customized approach or a tried-and-true methodology?
14. Do you speak to groups about the topic?
15. Have you written any articles or do you have a blog? Do you teach? Or is there something else you do that demonstrates your expertise on the subject?
16. What do you do to stay current on the topics of productivity and time management?
17. What is your preferred way to communicate with me? What's the best way to reach you—the phone, e-mail, or texting? How will you adapt if your preferred method isn't my preferred style (let's say I like e-mail better than a phone call)?
18. How will you tell me when I'm doing something wrong?
19. How can I be sure you're going to be honest and up front with me?

20. What are your relationship goals for working with a new client?
21. What is your fee structure?
22. What forms of payments do you accept?
23. Will I be working with you directly or someone else from your company?
24. What is your confidentiality policy?
25. Do you have a contract I can review?
26. Do you have a code of ethics?

Before you interview candidates, think about what you want the relationship to look like. How much do you want to pay? How often would you like to meet? What do you want to accomplish and how long do you want it to take? Compile the questions that will help you define the position you want filled.

CERTIFIED PROFESSIONAL ORGANIZERS® (CPOS)

Many productivity consultants go into the profession because it is a skill they are good at. The field has a low cost of entry and flexible hours, so it is easy to fit into a busy lifestyle. Going into a profession because you have good skills doesn't always translate into being successful training others. There's an easy method of screening out those coming into the field from the perspective of teaching what they know rather than what is best for you, and that is to ask whether they have any certifications.

The largest association for organizers and productivity professionals is the National Association of Professional Organizers (NAPO). NAPO is an important affiliation for serious professionals to have because it is where they learn about the many productivity tools that are available. Members share a great deal of information among themselves. There is an e-mail Listserv for asking and answering questions as well as providing resources to use with clients. There are more than

4,000 members worldwide in addition to regional and local chapters across the country. NAPO members are serious about their business and committed to education and learning. Another benefit of hiring someone who is a NAPO member is that all members have to abide by the NAPO code of ethics. Those ethics include maintaining anonymity and confidentiality for all clients. Even when they communicate with each other or ask for resources or discuss being baffled by a client experience, there is no mention of names, location, or any other identifying information.

Another important affiliation is to be a Certified Professional Organizer (CPO). The Board of Certification for Professional Organizers (BCPO) is a separate nonprofit organization, independent of NAPO, that credentials professional organizers and productivity professionals through an exam. To qualify for the exam, candidates must have 1,500 hours of client consulting experience, for which they've been paid, within a three-year time frame. In lieu of 1,500 hours, there are other ways of satisfying the requirement. But the goal is for CPOs to have on-site organizing, coaching, consultant, and training experience that demonstrates transfer of skills to clients. The exam is for people who make organizing and productivity improvement their most important career. The exam prerequisites work to exclude people who do this work part-time or as a hobby. Only those who are serious about their business, growing their business, and reaching that next level of professionalism will be certified.

If you are interviewing candidates who do not have certification, you can ask about their education. What kinds of courses have they taken? Have they attended conferences? How do they keep up with trends in the industry? While people who have certification show a propensity for continuing education in their field, individuals who are self-motivated, do the research, or are active in their local chapters might be just as well informed and on top of trends and the latest techniques.

REFERENCES AND REFERRALS

Your organizer or productivity consultant candidates should offer to provide you with references. If they don't bring it up, you should feel comfortable asking, "Do you have any references I can call? Are there past clients you've worked with, achieved success with, I can contact to ask about their experience working with you?"

Candidates should provide at least three references, especially if they specialize in an industry similar to yours. Obviously, candidates are only going to give you references for clients that they have had a successful relationship with. Even so, by probing with questions, you should be able to find out whether the type of relationship or the diversity of their relationships will work for you. Remember, you're looking for a consultant who is the right match for you.

When you speak to the references, here are ten important questions to ask to determine the commitment level and professionalism of the candidates you are interviewing:

1. Did they stay committed to the project?
2. Did they deliver advice and plans in a timely fashion?
3. Did you feel comfortable, at all times, sharing information with them?
4. Were they knowledgeable in their area of expertise and about productivity techniques?
5. How long was the relationship, and are you still working together? If not, why has the relationship ended?
6. What was your main goal in hiring a consultant?
7. Did you achieve that goal? And if not, do you feel you're on a good path to achieving that goal?
8. Did you feel the consultant was always being honest and straightforward with you? Ask for an example of a situation where the

consultant had to give some difficult feedback. How did the consultant deliver that feedback?

9. Did you ever feel intimidated by the kind of systems you were asked to implement? How did you overcome and implement the systems?

10. Of all the new procedures or processes you implemented, what has improved your situation the most?

Always check references. There is more you can learn beyond the positive relationship between the client and consultant. You are looking for a relationship that works for you. If you know you need someone who is completely honest and drives you to complete goals, ask about the consultant's operating style. If you know you cannot work with someone who is intimidating and need someone who is encouraging and uplifting, ask how the client felt after each meeting with the consultant. If you want a short-term relationship, ask about the goals the client and consultant set together and how long it took to reach them. If you want a long-term relationship, ask the client how long they have worked together and how they have set and achieved goals over that period. Note trends across clients. For you, it might be positive if the relationship is brief and successful vs. long and successful. There is much to be determined from an interview with past clients.

One of the primary ways people find productivity consultants is through referrals. But how do you know you can trust the referral? In this situation, interview your referral first, even before contacting the candidate. Hiring a productivity consultant isn't the same as hiring someone who is going to replace your kitchen cabinets. You want to find someone who will work well with you and help you accomplish your work and life goals. It might save you time in the end to screen out anyone who doesn't understand your needs or operating style.

RESOURCES TO FIND CONSULTANTS

Referrals from friends, associates, and colleagues are one of the best ways to find consultants. You can start by asking for referrals from other business associates, people from your local chamber of commerce, or other business networking groups. If you get a referral from someone you trust, there's a much higher likelihood that the person being referred to you is a great professional. If you don't come up with a number of personal referrals from trusted resources, the Internet is a great place to start your search. NAPO.net lists all its members along with their different specialties. You can search by country, zip code, and specialty.

When you elect to hire someone to help you navigate a path toward improved productivity, there are steps you can take to ensure the person you hire will create the right relationship with you. In the end, the right productivity consultant will not only help you achieve your goals, but also show you new insights and lead you to the realm of possibility.

PRODUCTIVITY POINTERS

If you choose to hire a consultant:

- Be prepared with the right questions.
- Know the attributes to look for that will be compatible with your preferences.
- Ask for referrals from friends and colleagues; it is one of the best ways to find a reputable consultant.

CHAPTER 14

CASE STUDY: JOHN ALLAIRE

You've met John in several chapters throughout the book as he and I tackled steps in improving his productivity. This account of his journey through the Peak Productivity Pyramid System tells the story from his perspective.

When he was thirteen years old, John Allaire read *The Art of the Deal*, by Donald Trump. Imagine the life of the successful real estate wheeler-dealer: helicopters and airplanes, penthouse suites, luxury hotel buildings. From that moment on, John knew exactly what he wanted to do when he grew up: deal in real estate.

As he puts it, "I was really blessed and fortunate to know at a very young age, here's the direction I want to go, here's the industry I want to be in, and of course there were the other benefits Trump suggested that would hopefully come with that."

During his time in college, John studied for and got his real estate license. During the following summer break, he went to work as the assistant to a top-producing agent in southeastern Massachusetts. He learned a great deal about listing and selling real estate working with a pro, and the experience helped launch him into his career. John completed his college education graduating magna cum laude with a degree in business management. After taking time off (thirty days, to be exact) in celebration of his graduation, he started his career in real estate, something he had waited to do for a decade. Rather than starting his own agency right away, John set a five-year plan to work for another agency, learning everything he could about the business. He worked for an independent company, rather than one of the name franchises.

On the fifth anniversary of his starting date in real estate, John left the established agency and started his own, Easton Real Estate. John was realizing his dream. As he explains, "I got into the residential real estate business. It was a great deal of fun, not only because I was learning so much, but also because of the energy. It was exciting; it was invigorating. Luckily, I didn't need any sleep because I didn't get much. I was probably putting in anywhere from sixteen- to twenty-hour days, six to seven days a week, for that first year when I opened my own company."

When he opened his businesses, he hired two other full-time employees. One person did all the roadwork: putting up and taking down signs, taking photographs, recording room measurements, currying documents to other places, and doing different things on the road. The other person worked in-house. This person was someone John had personally trained in all aspects of real estate so that she could run the office effectively. John was the only active real estate agent, primarily because he did not feel right about recruiting people from the agency he had worked at for the previous five years.

He started his business in 1998, and right through to 2005 the market was strong and inclining, which contributed to his early success. He rode a very nice wave of profitable real estate during the challenging first years of starting and learning how to run a business. During that time he proceeded to hire twelve agents and an additional two full-time and two part-time staff members. The agency was thriving, expanding, and completely filled the large office space.

WHEN THE BUBBLE BURST

Then, in 2005 and 2006, the real estate bubble burst and everything changed. As John puts it, "I don't want to say it was a disaster, but it wasn't pretty."

As he was figuring out what to do in this new real estate climate, the 2008 financial meltdown hit and created an economic crisis. Real estate had had such a rapid incline of increasing values and corresponding company profitability that when it stopped, the pendulum swung so hard in the other direction that it suddenly made business very difficult.

John reflects on that time: "Thank goodness I knew what I wanted to do for my career because it would have been really easy to get out of the business," he says. "If I liked real estate [only] because I was making some money, well, then, there's a decent likelihood that I would have just gotten out of the business, as many real estate agents and brokers have. I wanted to see it through, but it was only because it had always been my passion. So I said to myself, 'Whether it's good or bad, this is what I'm doing. So here we are; what do we do?'"

When things first get bad you don't notice as much. "It's always easy to think you're great," John says. "I had been running a successful real estate business for seven or eight years. But you learn very little when your business is running successfully. When the business actually starts to have problems, major problems or serious issues, that's when you learn the most. It is when you're stretched that eventually you say to yourself, 'What other resources are there? How do I solve these problems that I've never had before? I've been [doing] great for seven years, so what's going on?' You just don't have your feet under you because the scenery has changed, and the floor beneath you has changed, and so you have to figure out what to do to initially survive and then try and get back to 'thrivability.' I'll make up my own word," he adds.

John remembers that initially, in 2006 to 2007, he was trying to figure out if it was just a small downturn with the market improving in another two months. As he explains, "Of course, you have all these different reasons as to why it's so slow: We have to wait for the kids to get out of school; we have to wait for the kids to start school. We start finding all these external hopes to [explain] what will change the market.

"And then as it continues in a negative direction, you start to realize it's not going to be when the kids go back to school or when the bad winter is over—you're actually in a bad market and you have to figure out what to do," he says. "It also became clear that something needed to change or be done differently when we went from twelve real estate agents and six staff [members], down to three real estate agents and two staff. Many of the agents weren't surviving and found reasons to go other places, but staff just had to be laid off because the amount of business was no longer there to support [employing] them."

According to John, "That's when it really starts to have an impact, not just financially but emotionally, because now you're laying people off that you care about who have helped you, friends you've worked with for years. You have to let them go because you have no other option. If you don't, eventually everybody will have to go because the business will close. So you start to make these really difficult decisions about when and how and who.

"In retrospect," John continues, "I've learned that business owners, at least the newer ones, are quick to hire and slow to fire or lay off, because of those emotions, because you're waiting and hoping it will turn around. While all you're really doing is draining the resources of the company because you're emotionally attached to the people that have worked for you."

Eventually, John's company downsized, but even then, he says, "We still had a lot of overhead: the same office space and general expenses. We were still bleeding money and needing to turn things around."

It was around that time that John was coming up for air, determined to crawl out from under whatever this business downturn was. John is a master of staying in touch, and he got in contact with me. I was glad for the outreach as I was in the process of moving my business from organizing individual households to improving efficiencies and productivity for small businesses. I knew John would be a great source of contacts and introductions. As I started to describe my new business direction, John said, "I've always been a big fan of efficiencies. Maybe we should have a conversation about what I could do to improve the efficiencies in my organization."

With fewer employees and a smaller real estate market, but with the same space and overhead, John realized there were areas for improvement if the business was to survive. And he wanted more than survival; he coined his own word for what he wanted: *thrivability*. He wanted to figure out how to handle a business during an economic downturn. Until that time in his career, he had not experienced a down market, a difficult market, or a difficult economic climate. He discovered he hadn't learned very much those first seven years when business was easy and growing.

STEPPING UP THE PEAK PRODUCTIVITY PYRAMID

As we achieved improvements in his electronic and environmental organizational skills, John started to consult with me as a resource; I was someone he could work with in confidence and share ideas. He saw his company become more efficient and more organized, which helped save him money and time. For John, saving time in many respects was even more valuable than the money because having more time allowed him to think clearly. He was no longer so busy that he couldn't focus on macro problems or the bigger picture. In the first seven years he had been running the operations, getting to the next day, helping all of the staff and real estate agents with their problems; he really didn't have much need for strategic thinking. He didn't need to because the business was doing so well up to that point. For the next few years, during the start of the economic downturn, he had been mired in the details of day-to-day operations, just trying to survive. Having an additional block of time allowed him to start to strategize and do more CEO-level thinking.

As John moved into this strategic thinking mode, our conversation moved from talking about improving day-to-day efficiencies and time-saving measures to strategies. John describes the shift this way: "I don't know how to put it except to say, as Tamara listened to my strategic thinking, she helped me take it one step further, which was really fun. We began to brainstorm, and we started to change the business and take it to a different place—not only the business, but my personal career and the way I ran my business, my career in general, and then truly my life. And I don't believe I'm overstating that transition in any way."

This is where the Peak Productivity Pyramid System thrives. As John implemented organizational efficiencies to find time for strategic thinking, we started to work on goals for other aspects of his business and personal life and then aligned those goals with activities that would help him achieve his goals. Until this time, John had been focused almost exclusively on his business. Because his life was no longer consumed by his business, he was open to a journey that would take his personal life in new directions as well.

As John describes the experience, "When you turn forty years old, which I did in 2008, that's one of those key times when you start to look back on what has been your career up to this point, where you've been and what you've been doing. You start to question a lot of things, right? So I didn't go out and buy the red sports car or anything like that, and I wouldn't call it a midlife crisis, but a time for reflection. It's time to say here are those first forty years. What are the next forty [going to be] like, God willing, I get to live them?"

In addition to his business goals, John established personal goals and activities to help him stay physically well and healthy. He wanted time for emotional well-being, which he describes as time to be still or quiet. He preferred to have time for family, friends, a girlfriend, and eventually a wife.

Now he goes to the gym three to four times a week. There is more time for family and friends. There is at least a small block of time daily where he can just be still. According to John:

"When you run a business and have responsibility for employees, profits, and expenses, you need to do business throughout the year. So to be able to be still for a little bit or just to be quiet is a blessing. But what happens, and is really wonderful, is it all ties together. When you start to look at business efficiencies and strategies and start to tie in all of these other goals and activities, they all affect each other.

"Now, the ability to have quiet time or to serve others makes me a better businessman. It actually makes me a better boss; at least I hope it does. It helps me to run the company better because I have peace; [I've discovered] a stillness, that no matter what's going on around me, it's okay. There's no panic, even though business in real estate is still very challenging right now, but I am at ease, especially if you compare my emotional and spiritual state from five or six years [ago]. The market is still extremely challenging and difficult, but there is an internal calmness that, as the MasterCard commercial says, is priceless; it's worth millions and millions of dollars.

"My faith had always been important, but especially in the last three years, my relationship with God has grown immensely, and a big part of that has been because of the time I've [found] available to me, through Tamara's help. I've been extremely active in church, whether it's leading Bible studies or leading life communities, helping young adults mostly between the ages of twenty to thirty years old on their journey, their faith walk. And over the last couple of years a number of men have asked me for mentorship to help them walk through their life, whether it's personally in their relationships or in their work life. I've only had that opportunity to serve because of the things that have changed at my business. It's really an amazing thing that God has done and is doing where that time has allowed me to serve people."

If you recall, when John thought about what was possible for his future when he was thirteen years old, the idea was to have helicopters and his own 747 Boeing jet, if not an entire airline, and a couple of high-rise towers, just like Donald Trump. He has since flipped that vision of the possibilities for his future on its head.

"I'm certainly thankful for all of the success of my life, and the blessings, and what is certainly a good income, but what I'm really thankful for is the ability to serve," he says.

AFTERWORD

The difference between success and failure can be expressed in five words: I did not have time.

—Anonymous

I like to end my workshops on productivity with this quote. Often, people are overwhelmed taking in all the knowledge that they learn in the short time we are together. I like to leave them with a powerful piece of actionable information that they can apply to their day-to-day lives and that can transform their relationship with time. It is a fitting way to end this book as well.

Hopefully you have learned at least a handful of new techniques and actionable ideas from this book. Most important, you have learned a new framework to take you on your journey to achieving maximum productivity. Even if you decide that some of the techniques aren't right for you, you now have a roadmap to guide your path through all the levels of the Peak Productivity Pyramid. The more you study personal productivity, the better your techniques to achieve excellence within each level will become, leading you to start living in a world of possibility.

But before you can start making changes, it is critical that you shift your perception of time. The truth is that we all have time. Time is the greatest common denominator because regardless of gender, social class, or race, we all have the same exact amount of time. We all have twenty-four hours per day, and the choices we make with the time we have is what will make us successful. Remember, time management is choice management. So here is a simple exercise to get you started on your journey to possibility:

For the next week, before you start implementing any of the other tips and techniques that you have learned, I would like you to commit to not using the words "have" and "time" together. I want you to take ownership of your choices regarding your time and instead use expressions like, "I had more important tasks on my list," or "I have other priorities." The point is for you to start living in the realm of choice management and not time management. The other pieces will be much easier to implement and your journey to peak productivity will be a much smoother one. Here's to a more productive you!

ABOUT THE AUTHOR

Tamara Myles, a Certified Professional Organizer® (CPO), is dedicated to helping entrepreneurs and corporate clients live a life with purpose, enabling them to be all they can and dream of becoming.

Over the years, she has evolved from a hands-on organizer to productivity expert and business consultant. Her business evolution was a direct result of discovering that disarray within one's electronic and physical space is often a symptom of larger problems. To help her clients, Tamara developed a more comprehensive approach than any that exists on the market or in the literature: a proprietary framework, the Peak Productivity Pyramid™ System. The Peak Productivity Pyramid System starts with physical and electronic organization as building blocks, then looks at time management systems and personal and business goals to increase productivity. Finally, the Peak Productivity Pyramid System challenges clients to create goals that will enhance their businesses and fulfill their lives.

She is a professional speaker and productivity trainer, conducting webinars and in-person training for individual and corporate clients that include Anytime Fitness and Best Buy.

Before starting her own business, Tamara was an advertising executive where she managed exciting projects for several prestigious brands, including CoverGirl, Adidas, Sony Electronics, Lands' End, Spiegel, and many more. Her experience managing multimillion-dollar advertising projects demanded her inherent organization and productivity skills. During her fast-track career, Tamara was continually praised for her ability to organize space, documents, people, and time lines. Many of her habits became the model for others within her firm to follow, which enabled them to continually exceed client expectations.

As a native of Brazil, Tamara first came to the United States on a college scholarship and graduated from Southern Illinois University, receiving a degree in communications with highest honors. She is fluent in English and Portuguese, and proficient in French and Spanish.

Tamara is a member of the Women's Business Network of Southeastern Massachusetts (WBNSEMA), Northeast Human Resources Association (NEHRA), the National Association of Professional Organizers (NAPO), and NAPO-New England, where she served on the board of directors as vice president. She lives in New England with her husband and three children.

NOTES

CHAPTER 3 (PHYSICAL ORGANIZATION)

1. CareerBuilder.com, "Being Perceived as a Hoarder May Cost Workers a Promotion, Finds New CareerBuilder Survey," press release, July 21, 2011.

CHAPTER 4 (ELECTRONIC ORGANIZATION)

1. "Drowning in Email, Photos, Files? Hoarding Goes Digital," *Wall Street Journal,* March 27, 2012.
2. Susan Feldman, *Hidden Costs of Information Work: A Progress Report*, IDC Report #217936, May 6, 2009.
3. "Email Addiction Results Are In," AOL survey, http://cdn.web-mail.aol.com/survey/aol/en-us/index.htm (accessed September 12, 2009).
4. Tony Schwartz, "Breaking the Email Addiction," *HRB Blog Network,* June 29, 2010, http://blogs.hbr.org/schwartz/2010/06/breaking-the-email-addiction.html (accessed March 21, 2013).

5. "Information Overload: Now $900 Billion—What Is Your Organization's Exposure?" *Basex: TechWatch*, http://www.basexblog.com/2008/12/19/information-overload-now-900-billion-what-is-your-organizations-exposure/.

CHAPTER 5 (TIME MANAGEMENT)

1. Jason Fried and David Heinemeier Hansson, *Rework* (New York: Crown Business, 2010), 23–25.
2. Harold L. Taylor, *Making Time Work for You: A Guide Book to Effective and Productive Time Management* (New York: Beaufort, 1981).
3. Vince Poscente, *The Age of Speed: Learning to Thrive in a More-Faster-Now World* (New York: Ballantine Books, 2008), 19.

CHAPTER 6 (PLAN)

1. Harold L. Taylor, *Making Time Work for You: A Guide Book to Effective and Productive Time Management* (New York: Beaufort, 1981).
2. David Allen, *Getting Things Done* (New York: Penguin Putnam, 2001).

CHAPTER 8 (PERFORM)

1. Brian Tracy, *Eat That Frog! 21 Great Ways to Stop Procrastinating and Get More Done in Less Time* (San Francisco: Berrett-Koehler Publishers, 2007), 3.
2. Neil Fiore, *The Now Habit: A Strategic Program for Overcoming Procrastination and Enjoying Guilt-Free Play* (New York: Tarcher, 2007), 62–67.

CHAPTER 10 (PAVING THE WAY TO POSSIBILITY)

1. Brian Tracy, *No Excuses: The Power of Self-Discipline* (New York: Vanguard Press, 2010), 6.

2. Teresa Amabile and Steven Kramer, "Do Happier People Work Harder?" *New York Times*, September 3, 2011.

3. "Health and Productivity Among U.S. Workers," Karen Davis, Ph.D., Sara R. Collins, Ph.D., Michelle M. Doty, Ph.D., Alice Ho, and Alyssa L. Holmgren, The Commonwealth Fund, August 2005.

4. National Sleep Foundation, "Longer Work Days Leave Americans Nodding Off On the Job," press release, March 3, 2008.

5. R. Z. Goetzel et al., "Health, Absence, Disability, and Presenteeism Cost Estimates of Certain Physical and Mental Health Conditions Affecting US Employers," *Journal of Occupational and Environmental Medicine* 46 (April 2004), 398–412.

6. Harold L. Taylor, *Slowing Down the Speed of Life: A Holistic Approach to Time Management* (Harold Taylor Time Consultants, 2010).

7. Tony Schwartz, "Relax! You'll Be More Productive," *New York Times,* February 9, 2013, http://www.nytimes.com/2013/02/10/opinion/sunday/relax-youll-be-more-productive. html?pagewanted=all&_r=0 (accessed March 23, 2013).

CHAPTER 11 (POSSIBILITY)

1. Janet A. Simons, Donald B. Irwin, and Beverly A. Drinnien, *Psychology: The Search for Understanding* (New York: West Publishing, 1987).

2. Ibid.

CHAPTER 12 (POWER OFFICE)

1. Harold Taylor, "Efficiency vs. Effectiveness," https://www.taylor intime.com/index.php?option=com_content&view=article&id= 722:efficiency-vs-effectiveness&catid=71:personal-productivity& Itemid=200106# (accessed October 10, 2012).

INDEX